ongress Cataloging-in-Publication Data

arol Ann Caprione, 1950–
ties in restaurant careers / Carol Ann Caprione

— (VGM opportunities series)
42-8662-1 : $11.95. — ISBN 0-8442-8664-8 (pbk.) : $11.95
rvice—Vocational guidance—United States.   I. Title.

2C46   1989
—dc20   89-37224
                                            CIP

M Career Horizons, a division of NTC Publishing Group.
Publishing Group, 4255 West Touhy Avenue,
hicago), Illinois 60646-1975 U.S.A.

VGM Opportunities Series

OPPORTUNI
RESTAURAN
CAREERS

Carol Ann C
Chmelynski

Foreword by
Harris H. Rusitzky
President
National Restaurant Associa

REGIONA

VGM Career
a division of *NTC P*
Lincolnwood, Illinois

Cover Pho
Front cover
photos cour
lower left,
photo; lowe
Back cover:
and lower ri
lower left, F

Library of C

Chmelynski, C
Opportuni
Chmelynski
p. cm.
ISBN 0-8
1. Food se
II. Series.
TX911.3.V6
647.95'023'73

Published by VG
© 1990 by NTC
Lincolnwood (C
All rights reserv
in a retrieval syst
electronic, mech
the prior permiss
Manufactured in
9 0 VP 9 8 7 6 5

ABOUT THE AUTHOR

Carol Ann Caprione Chmelynski began her food service career in 1976 with the National Milk Producers Federation. She went on to become an editorial assistant at the Food Marketing Institute and later worked as a communications specialist at the National Restaurant Association in Washington, D.C., where she wrote feature articles for the association's monthly magazine, *NRA News*. That magazine is now titled *Restaurants USA*.

Mrs. Chmelynski worked as a copywriter for the advertising firm of Stackig, Sanderson and White in McLean, Virginia, where she wrote product as well as job recruitment ads for high technology companies such as Electronic Data Systems, Network Solutions, Tempest Technologies, and Capital Systems Group, Inc.

Currently, Mrs. Chmelynski is the assistant managing editor of *School Board News,* a biweekly newspaper of the National School Board Association in Alexandria, Virginia.

Opportunities in Restaurant Careers is Mrs. Chmelynski's second book in the VGM Opportunities series. Her first book, *Opportunities in Food Services,* was published in 1984.

FOREWORD

There has never been a better time to embark on a career in the food service industry. The demographics tell the story. In the 1990s, our industry will need 1.3 million more people to meet our growth projections. That means that by 1995 we will need nearly ten million employees, or, phrased another way, our industry will employ one out of nine working Americans to maintain growth.

This need for new employees bodes well for people entering the industry; it means there is tremendous opportunity for growth, advancement, increased responsibility, financial rewards, job satisfaction—all those things that accompany success for people who are on a food service career path. The breadth and depth of our industry is unparalleled by any other industry that I know of. There are a great number of sectors in the industry—table service, fast food, institutional feeders, catering, and many more; the variety of positions with different responsibilities that each sector offers is remarkable. People with all kinds of tastes and talents will find the perfect position in food service.

The stories about young people with little capital who commit themselves to food service and rise rapidly are very common, and they relate to a real pattern in our industry. The owner-operator of a successful restaurant and the executive in the headquarters of a large chain often started out in a busing or dishwashing slot. In no other industry can people scale the ladder of advancement so rapidly. They are limited only by their own imagination. Success is there for the taking for those who genuinely enjoy dealing with people and who are willing to work hard.

Harris H. Rusitzky
President
National Restaurant Association

CONTENTS

Restaurants today serve as both a convenience and a form of enjoyment.
(Hyatt Regency photo)

CHAPTER 1

AN OVERVIEW OF THE RESTAURANT INDUSTRY

Restaurants play an important role today, providing a convenience for busy two-career families and a means of entertainment for those who enjoy having other people prepare and serve food to them. Restaurants were originally established as a necessary option for people who had to be away from home and couldn't use their own kitchens. Still serving that purpose today, restaurants also are used by people who want to eliminate the chores of food shopping, preparation, and cleanup.

TYPES OF RESTAURANTS

There are many different types of eating establishments, including cafeterias, carryout operations, coffee shops, drugstore counters, fast food chains, sandwich shops, and white tablecloth operations. Some of the different types of restaurants include:

- *Family restaurant.* As the name implies, one would come to this restaurant with children, spouse, or friends for a casual meal in a relaxed, unpretentious atmosphere. Denny's, Red Lobster, and Pizza Hut are all family restaurants.

- *Atmosphere restaurant.* The setting, decor, historic context, special artifacts, or view sets the atmosphere for this type of restaurant, which is usually visited for a special reason. The dress is sometimes a little more formal than at a family restaurant. The Hard Rock Cafe restaurants, with their collections of memorabilia from the music world, are atmosphere restaurants.
- *Gourmet restaurant.* The food, service, and gracious atmosphere all add to a relaxed dining experience at this type of restaurant. It is more formal than the family or atmosphere restaurant, and it is characterized by an unhurried pace. Credit cards are accepted here, and beer, wine, and liquor are offered. Often restaurants serving cuisines from other countries, such as France, Japan, and Italy, are gourmet restaurants.
- *Fast food restaurant.* This type of restaurant primarily sells limited lines of beverages and prepared food items, such as fish, hamburger, chicken, or roast beef sandwiches, for consumption either on or near the premises or to take home. Fast food restaurants are inexpensive, appeal to all ages, and are suitable for snack service as well as meal service. Seating is available, but customers are not served. Food is ordered and picked up at the counter. McDonald's and Burger King are two of the most successful fast food restaurant chains.
- *Cafeterias.* Customers make food and beverage selections from a wide display of items. There may be some limited waiter or waitress service. Tables and/or booths are usually provided. Ponderosa and Bonanza are two well-known cafeteria-style restaurant chains.
- *Take-out restaurant.* Food is purchased and taken off the premises—no seating is offered. Sometimes, home delivery

is available. Domino's Pizza is a take-out restaurant franchise.

These groupings are to some extent arbitrary, as restaurant categories rarely have neat, sharp boundaries.

The NDP CREST Association (food service industry specialists) breaks the commercial food service industry into the following three segments:

Quick Service Segment

> Restaurant is perceived as fast food/take out.
> Food specialty is pizza, ice cream, chicken, or doughnuts.

Midscale Segment

> If the restaurant has not been placed in the quick service segment or upscale segment, it is classified as midscale.
> Restaurant may, but is not required to, accept credit cards, serve beer, wine, or alcohol.

Upscale Segment

> Restaurant is not perceived as fast food/take out.
> Credit cards are accepted.
> Full liquor service, including beer, wine, and alcohol is offered.

AN EXPANDING FUNCTION

In recent years, Americans have come to view restaurant dining as an enjoyable event. People are going out to eat for nourishment, to be sure, but they also frequent restaurants for the experience. They want to be entertained, to have an adventure, and to try something new.

Dinner in a restaurant—once just a prelude to a movie or an aftermath to a play—has now become the theater. Dining out has become the show.

A VIABLE CAREER OPPORTUNITY

The expanding importance of restaurants in American lifestyles is good news for those seeking a job in the restaurant industry. Here are ten good reasons to consider the restaurant industry when setting career goals.

1. The restaurant industry employs more than six million people, making it the number-one retail employer in America.
2. The restaurant industry ranks number one in the total number of business units.
3. The restaurant industry will need about 175,000 new employees each year to keep pace with the growing demand for services.
4. The restaurant industry continues to grow through both good and bad economic times.
5. The restaurant industry serves food to nearly 200 million customers each month.
6. Americans eat in restaurants an average of 3.7 times a week, or 192 times a year.
7. The restaurant industry is the fourth-largest retail industry in the country.
8. Managerial and management-related workers employed in

eating and drinking places will increase over 50 percent from 1986 to 2000.

9. In the United States, there are about 380,000 restaurants available to the public.

10. More than 575,000 individuals are employed in a supervisory capacity in eating and drinking places, a 47 percent increase since 1980.

These ten facts about the restaurant industry can mean personal growth and opportunity for qualified, energetic people. That is why restaurant workers make up one of the largest and fastest-growing occupational groups in the nation's labor force.

Job opportunities exist almost everywhere for almost any interested person, including those with limited skills and little formal education.

The restaurant industry is one of the very few industries left that still give unskilled workers a chance to start at the bottom and work their way up. Of course, the amount of career preparation in both formal and on-the-job training determines the level of entry into the field. But restaurants offer plenty of room for upward mobility, and people who are willing to make a personal investment in their success are practically guaranteed a good spot.

SUCCEEDING IN THE INDUSTRY

A career in the restaurant industry can be one of the most rewarding ones available, but it will also be one of the most demanding. People who are successful in the restaurant industry all possess several important qualities that contribute to their advancement. These qualities include:

- *Positive work attitude.* This begins with punctuality, pride in personal appearance, and a professional manner. In addition, a good attitude means an eagerness to learn, a willingness to work, and an ability to accept constructive criticism and direction.
- *Intelligence and ambition.* The restaurant industry has a need and a place for people at all job levels. Therefore, opportunities to gain experience and on-the-job, as well as academic, training are excellent. Individuals who display the ambition to use these opportunities as stepping-stones to advancement and who also possess the intelligence to gain the maximum benefit from their training and experience are sure to succeed.
- *Physical and mental health.* Every restaurant job involves peak periods and deadlines leading up to them. Pressures can be intense; intermittent workloads can be heavy. Therefore, good physical health is a must. A healthy mental outlook that enables the individual to function well with fellow workers and serve the public effectively is also necessary.

GROWTH IN GOOD TIMES AND BAD

Economic fluctuations can affect every industry. However, the most noticeable effect of the recent economic downturns on the restaurant industry has been a slowing in its rate of growth. During downturns, restaurant sales volume has continued to rise, and so has employment.

The restaurant industry is one that offers excellent security potential for the long term because it has almost always had more jobs than people to fill them. Its healthy growth performance indicates that this situation is likely to continue into the future. Also, because food is such a basic staple and food consumption away from home is so vital to America's way of life, the industry is guaranteed a stable future as the nation's mobility and work force grow.

Top: Waiters and waitresses take customers' orders, serve food and beverages, prepare checks, and sometimes accept payment. (Hilton International photo) *Bottom:* Fast food workers gain valuable experience that can help them move up in the restaurant industry. (Kentucky Fried Chicken photo)

CHAPTER 2

ENTRY-LEVEL RESTAURANT WORKERS

The restaurant industry is one of those rare fields that offer a wide range of opportunities to people at all levels of educational attainment. Almost any interested person, including people who have limited skills or little formal education, can find a niche in this growing industry.

The industry has opportunities for virtually people of all working ages. For sixteen-year-old high school students or for those who are beginning or changing a career later in life, a career in the restaurant industry can prove to be an excellent choice.

JOBS REQUIRING MINIMAL TRAINING

Buspersons

Buspersons clear and reset tables with fresh linen and silverware; they refill water glasses and assist waiters and waitresses in serving and housekeeping chores in the dining area. Many people who now enjoy high-level management positions in the restaurant industry have started their careers as buspersons.

Waiters and Waitresses

Waiters and waitresses take customers' orders, serve food and beverages, prepare itemized checks, and sometimes accept payment. However, the manner in which they perform these tasks varies considerably, depending on the type of restaurant establishment in which they work. In coffee shops, for example, they are expected to provide fast and efficient, yet courteous, service.

In fine restaurants, where gourmet meals are accompanied by attentive formal service, waiters and waitresses serve the meal at a more leisurely pace and offer more personal service to patrons. For example, they might recommend a certain kind of wine as a complement to a particular entree, explain how various items on the menu are prepared, or prepare some salads and other special dishes right at the table.

Depending on the type of restaurant, waiters and waitresses might be required to perform duties associated with other food and beverage service occupations in addition to waiting on tables. Some of these tasks might include escorting guests to tables, serving customers seated at counters, setting up and clearing tables, or operating the cash register. In larger or more formal restaurants, however, waiters and waitresses usually are not required to perform these duties.

Waiters and waitresses are critical to any type of restaurant. They must like dealing with people and be poised and efficient under the stress of simultaneous demands.

Hosts and Hostesses

Hosts and hostesses are responsible for evoking a good impression of the restaurant by warmly welcoming guests. In a courteous manner, they direct patrons to where they may leave their coats and other personal items and show patrons where they may wait until their table is ready. Hosts and hostesses assign guests to tables suitable for the size of their group, escort them to their seats, and provide menus.

As restaurants' personal representatives to patrons, hosts and hostesses must try to ensure that service is prompt and courteous and the meal is enjoyable. They also ensure order and cleanliness and adjust any complaints dissatisfied diners might have. Hosts and hostesses schedule dining reservations, arrange parties, and organize any special services that are required. In some restaurants, they also perform cashier duties.

Sanitation/Maintenance Employees

Sanitation/maintenance employees ensure that walls and floors are clean and that there is a steady flow of clean cooking equipment, utensils, dishware, and silver. Most modern restaurants have dishwashers and other machines to assist in performing these tasks. Although the job does not sound glamorous, sanitation and maintenance employees are vital to the operation of any restaurant.

Dining Room Attendants and Bartender's Assistants

Dining room attendants and bartender's assistants help waiters, waitresses, and bartenders by keeping the serving area stocked with supplies, cleaning tables, and removing dirty dishes. They replenish the supply of clean linen, dishes, silverware, and glasses in the restaurant dining room and keep the bar stocked with glasses, liquor, ice, and drink garnishes. Bartender's helpers also keep the bar equipment clean and wash glasses. Dining room attendants set tables with clean tablecloths, napkins, silverware, glasses, and dishes and serve ice water, rolls, and butter to patrons.

At the end of the meal, dining room attendants remove dirty dishes and soiled linens from the tables and take them to the kitchen. Cafeteria attendants stock serving tables with food, trays, dishes, and silverware and sometimes carry trays to dining tables for patrons.

Counter Attendants

Counter attendants take orders and serve food at counters. In cafeterias, they serve food displayed on counters and steam tables as requested by patrons, carve meat, dish out vegetables, ladle sauces and soups, and fill cups and glasses.

In lunchrooms and coffee shops, a counter attendant takes orders from customers seated at the counter, transmits the orders to the kitchen, and picks up and serves the food when it is ready. They also fill cups and glasses with coffee, soda, and other beverages and prepare fountain specialties such as milk shakes and ice cream sundaes. Often counter attendants prepare short-order items such as sandwiches and salads and wrap or place orders in containers to be taken out and consumed elsewhere. In addition, counter attendants write up itemized checks and accept payment.

Fast Food Workers

Fast food workers take orders from customers standing at counters at fast food restaurants. They gather the ordered beverage and food items from the stock waiting to be sold, serve them to the customer, and accept payment. Many fast food workers also cook and package french fries, make coffee, and fill beverage cups using a drink-dispensing machine.

WORKING CONDITIONS

Restaurant workers are on their feet most of the time and often have to carry heavy trays of food, dishes, and glassware. During busy dining periods, they are under pressure to serve customers quickly and efficiently. The work is relatively safe, but care must be taken to avoid slips and falls or burns.

Although some restaurant employees work forty hours or more a week, the majority are part time—a larger proportion than in almost any other occupation.

The majority of those working part-time schedules do so on a voluntary basis because the wide range in dining hours creates work opportunities attractive to homemakers, students, and others in need of supplemental income.

Many restaurant workers are expected to work evenings, weekends, and holidays. Some choose to work split shifts, meaning they work for several hours during the middle of the day, take a few hours off in the afternoon, and then return to their jobs for the evening hours.

EMPLOYMENT

Restaurant workers held 4.2 million jobs in 1986. Waiters and waitresses held 1.7 million of these jobs; fast food workers, 1.5 million; bartenders, 396,000; dining room and cafeteria attendants and bartender helpers, 433,000; and hosts and hostesses, 172,000. Restaurants, coffee shops, bars, and other retail eating and drinking places employed 80 percent of all food and beverage service workers. Of the remainder, nearly half worked in hotels and other lodging places. Others worked in bowling alleys, casinos, country clubs, and other membership organizations.

Jobs are located throughout the country but are most plentiful in large cities and tourist areas. Vacation resorts offer seasonal employment, and some workers alternate between summer and winter resorts instead of remaining in one area the entire year.

TRAINING

There are no specific educational requirements for restaurant jobs. Although many employers prefer to hire high school graduates for waiter and waitress and host and hostess positions, a high school diploma is usually not required for fast food workers, counter attendants, and dining room attendants and bartender's helpers. Many entrants to these jobs have little or no work experience.

OTHER QUALIFICATIONS

Restaurant employers place a high emphasis on personal qualities. Restaurant workers should be well spoken and have a neat and clean appearance because they are in close contact with the public. They should enjoy dealing with all kinds of people. A pleasant disposition and a sense of humor are important. State laws often require that restaurant workers obtain health certificates showing that they are free of contagious diseases.

Waiters and waitresses need a good memory to avoid confusing customers' orders and to recall the faces, names, and preferences of frequent patrons. They also should be good at arithmetic if they have to total bills without the aid of a calculator or cash register. In restaurants specializing in foreign foods, knowledge of a foreign language is helpful.

Experience waiting on tables is preferred by restaurants and hotels that have rigid table service standards. Jobs at these establishments often have higher earnings but might also require higher educational standards than less formal establishments.

Most restaurant workers acquire their skills on the job by observing and working with more experienced workers. Some employers, particularly in some fast food restaurants, use self-instruction programs to teach new employees food-preparation and service skills through the use of audiovisual presentations and instructional booklets.

Some public and private vocational schools, restaurant associations, and large restaurant chains also provide classroom training in a generalized food service curriculum.

ADVANCEMENT

Opportunities for advancement are limited in small restaurant establishments. After gaining some experience, some dining room and cafeteria attendants and bartender's helpers are able to advance to waiter, waitress, or bartender jobs.

Waiters and waitresses often advance by finding a job in a larger restaurant where prospects for tip earnings are better. Some hosts and hostesses and waiters and waitresses advance to supervisory jobs, such as maitre d'hotel, dining room supervisor, or restaurant manager.

JOB OUTLOOK

Job openings for restaurant workers are expected to be plentiful through the year 2000. Most openings will come about from the need to replace the high proportion of workers who leave this very large occupation each year. There is substantial movement into and out of these occupations because the limited formal education and training requirements for these jobs allow easy entry and the predominance of part-time jobs is attractive to persons seeking a short-term source of income rather than a career. Many of these workers move to other occupations; others stop working to assume household responsibilities or to attend school. Workers under the age of twenty-five have traditionally filled a significant number of these jobs. This pool of young workers is expected to shrink through the year 2000. This will force many employers to offer higher wages, better fringe benefits, and more training to attract and retain workers.

Employment of restaurant occupations is expected to grow much faster than the average for all occupations through the year 2000. The financial success of eating and drinking places is dependent on the overall rate of economic activity in the business world, such as workers' lunches and entertaining clients, so employment opportunities will increase with the growth of the economy. Demand also will stem from population growth, rising personal income, and increased leisure time.

Potential earnings are highest in popular restaurants and fine dining establishments. Therefore, these restaurants will experience keen competition for a limited number of jobs.

EARNINGS

Restaurant workers derive their earnings from a combination of hourly wages and customer tips. Their wages and the amount of tips they receive vary greatly, depending on the type of job and establishment.

For example, fast food workers and hosts and hostesses generally do not receive tips, so their wage requirement might be higher than that of waiters and waitresses, who might earn more from tips than wages. In some restaurants, waiters and waitresses contribute a portion of their tips to a pool, which is distributed among many of the establishment's other food and beverage service workers. This arrangement allows workers who normally do not receive tips, such as dining room attendants, to share in the rewards for a room well served.

In 1986, median hourly earning (including tips) of full-time waiters and waitresses was $4.30. The middle 50 percent earned between $3.33 and $5.90; the top 10 percent earned at least $7.77. For most waiters and waitresses, higher earnings are primarily the result of receiving more in tips rather than higher hourly wages. Tips usually average between 10 and 15 percent of guest's checks, so waiters and waitresses working in busy, expensive restaurants earn the highest wages.

Median hourly earnings (including tips) of full-time dining room attendants and bartender's helpers were $4.10 in 1986. The middle 50 percent earned between $3.45 and $5.10. Most received over half of their earnings as wages; the rest was their share of the proceeds from tip pools.

Full-time counter attendants and fast food workers had median hourly earnings (including any tips) of $3.80 in 1986. The middle 50 percent earned between $3.25 and $4.33, while the highest 10 percent earned more than $6.33. Although some counter attendants receive part of their earnings as tips, fast food workers generally do not.

Federal law permits employers to credit an employee's tip earnings toward the minimum hourly wage up to an amount equaling 40 percent of the minimum wage. Some employers exercise this right. Therefore, in 1986, an employer who claimed the full credit was permitted to pay a minimum wage of $2.01 an hour instead of the normal $3.35 an hour. Employers are also permitted to deduct from wages the cost, or fair value, of any meals or lodging provided. However, many employers provide free meals and furnish uniforms.

CHAPTER 3

MID-LEVEL POSITIONS

In the restaurant industry, job positions in the mid-level category vary considerably from one establishment to another. These positions generally require some experience. On-the-job training is usually provided for the recently hired.

BARTENDERS

Bartenders must be able to skillfully prepare a drink at a moment's notice. It might be a cool glass of gin and tonic or a colorful, exotic mixture such as a Singapore Sling. Bartenders make these drinks by combining, in exact proportions, ingredients selected from what might seem to be a bewildering variety of alcoholic beverages, mixes, and garnishes. A well-stocked bar contains dozens of types and brands of liquor, beer, and wine plus soft drinks, fruits and fruit juices, cream, soda, and tonic water.

Bartenders fill the drink orders that waiters and waitresses take from customers seated in the restaurant or lounge as well as orders from customers seated at the bar. Because some people like their cocktails made a specific way, bartenders occasionally are asked to mix drinks to suit customers' tastes. Most bartenders are required to know dozens of drink recipes and be able to mix drinks accurately, quickly, and without waste, even during the busiest periods. Therefore, an excellent memory is important.

Besides mixing and serving drinks, bartenders collect payment, operate the cash register, and clean up after customers have left. They may also serve food items to customers seated at the bar.

Bartenders who work at service bars have little contact with customers. They work at small bars in restaurants, hotels, and clubs where drinks are served only to diners at tables. However, the majority of bartenders work in eating and drinking establishments where they also directly serve and socialize with patrons.

Many establishments, especially larger ones, use automatic equipment to mix drinks of varying complexity at the push of a button. However, bartenders still must be efficient and knowledgeable so they can prepare drinks not handled by the automatic equipment or mix drinks when it is not functioning. Also, equipment is no substitute for the friendly socializing most customers prefer and expect.

Bartenders usually are responsible for ordering and maintaining an inventory of liquor, mixes, and other bar supplies. They also arrange the bottles and glassware into attractive displays and often wash glassware used at the bar.

Working Conditions

Many bartenders work more than forty hours per week; night work, weekend work, and split shifts are common. For many bartenders, however, the opportunity for friendly conversation with customers and the possibility of one day managing or owning a bar or restaurant of their own more than offset these disadvantages. For others, the opportunity to get part-time employment is important.

Because bartenders play a significant role in making an establishment attractive to customers, a pleasant, outgoing personality is a must for their career. In addition to understanding and liking all kinds of people, bartenders must have excellent memories for faces, names, and recipes. Many bartenders pride themselves on being able to fill any drink order without looking up a recipe and are able to mix and serve drinks with flair, a quality that helps make them popular with customers and employees alike.

Good bartenders must be able to work accurately and rapidly. Busy periods in popular establishments can create considerable pressure, making a cool efficiency, as well as attention to detail, an occupational necessity.

Because bartenders are required to stand for many hours, good physical condition is vital. Better-than-average strength is sometimes needed to lift heavy cases of liquor or mixes.

Generally, bartenders must be at least twenty-one years of age, and employers prefer to hire persons who are twenty-five or older.

Bartenders should be familiar with state and local laws concerning sales of alcoholic beverages.

Training

Some bartenders acquire their skills by attending a bartending school or taking vocational and technical school courses that include instruction on state and local laws and regulations, cocktail recipes, attire and conduct, and stocking a bar. Some of these schools help their graduates find jobs.

Earnings

Full-time bartenders had median hourly earnings (including tips) of $5.35 in 1986. The middle 50 percent earned from $4.08 to $7.18; the top 10 percent earned at least $9.75. Like waiters and waitresses, bartenders may receive more than half of their earnings in tips. Service bartenders are often paid higher hourly wages to offset their lower tip earnings.

CHEFS, COOKS, AND OTHER KITCHEN WORKERS

Cooks and chefs are the artists and the administrators of the restaurant industry. Some of the most creative and interesting jobs of the entire industry are performed by these people. There is a strong demand for talented, well-trained cooks and chefs throughout the country.

In 1986, about 2.6 million chefs and cooks were working in restaurants and other eating establishments. Some experts have predicted about fifty thousand job openings a year for cooks and chefs. Others have predicted as many as eighty-five thousand new job openings a year.

Nature of the Work

In any restaurant—whether it prides itself on home cooking or exotic foreign cuisine—chefs, cooks, and other kitchen workers largely are responsible for the reputation it acquires.

Some restaurants are famous for offering a varied menu featuring meals that are time consuming and difficult to prepare. These restaurants demand a highly skilled chef. Other restaurants emphasize fast service and offer hamburgers and sandwiches that can be prepared in advance or even in a few minutes by a fast food or short-order cook with only limited cooking skills.

Chefs and cooks are responsible for preparing meals that are tasty and attractively presented. Although the terms *chef* and *cook* are often used interchangeably, the professional chef generally is a far more skilled, trained, and experienced individual.

Many chefs have earned fame for both themselves and the restaurants, hotels, and institutions where they work because of their skill in artfully preparing the traditional favorites as well as creating new dishes and improving familiar ones.

Institutional chefs and cooks work in the kitchens of schools, industrial cafeterias, hospitals, and other institutions. For each meal, they prepare a small selection of entrées, vegetables, and desserts, but in large quantities and in huge kettles, not small pots.

Restaurant chefs and cooks generally prepare a wider selection of dishes for each meal, cooking most individual servings to order.

Whether they work in institutions or in restaurants, chefs and cooks measure, mix, and cook ingredients according to recipes. They use a variety of pots, pans, cutlery, and equipment including ovens, broilers, grills, slicers, grinders, and blenders in the course of their work.

In addition, chefs and cooks often are responsible for directing the work of other kitchen workers, estimating food requirements, and ordering food supplies. Some chefs and cooks also help plan meals and develop menus.

Bread and pastry bakers, called pastry chefs in some kitchens, produce baked goods for restaurants, institutions, and retail bakery shops. Unlike bakers, who work at large automated industrial bakeries, bread and pastry bakers need only supply the customers who visit their establishment. They bake smaller quantities of breads, rolls, pastries, pies, and cakes, doing most of the work by hand. They measure and mix ingredients, shape and bake the dough, and apply fillings and decorations.

Short-order cooks prepare foods to order in restaurants and coffee shops that specialize in fast service. They grill and garnish hamburgers, prepare sandwiches, fry eggs, and cook french fries, often working on several orders at the same time. Prior to busy periods, short-order cooks might slice meats and cheese or prepare coleslaw or potato salad. During slow periods, they might clean the grill as well as other food preparation surfaces and the counter.

In small establishments, such as diners, short-order cooks may serve people at the counter, collect payments, and operate the cash register.

Specialty fast food cooks are responsible for preparing a limited selection of menu items in fast food restaurants. They cook and package batches of food, such as hamburgers and fried chicken, which are prepared to order or kept warm until sold.

Other kitchen workers, under the direction of chefs and cooks, are responsible for performing tasks that require less skill. Their duties include weighing and measuring ingredients, fetching pots and pans, and stirring and straining soups and sauces. They clean; peel and slice potatoes, vegetables, and fruits; and make salads. They also might have to cut and grind meats, poultry, and seafood in preparation for cooking. They clean work areas, equipment, and utensils as well as dishes and silverware.

The number and types of workers employed in the kitchen depend partly on the size and kind of restaurant. Fast food outlets offer only a few items, which are prepared by fast food cooks. Smaller restaurants usually feature a limited number of easy-to-prepare items, supplemented by short-order specialties and ready-made desserts. Usually one chef or cook prepares all the food with the help of a short-order cook and one or two other kitchen workers.

Large eating places usually have more varied menus and prepare, from start to finish, more of the food they serve. Kitchen staffs often include several chefs or cooks, sometimes called assistant or apprentice chefs or cooks, a bread and pastry baker, and many less-skilled kitchen workers. Each cook or chef usually has a special assignment and often a special job title such as vegetable, fry, or sauce cook.

Executive chefs or head cooks coordinate the work of the kitchen staff and often direct certain kinds of food preparation. They decide the serving sizes, plan the menus, and buy the food supplies.

Working Conditions

Many restaurant and institutional kitchens have modern equipment, convenient work areas, and air conditioning; but others, particularly in older and smaller eating places, are not so well equipped. Other variations in working conditions depend on the type and quantity of food being prepared and the local laws governing food service operations.

Workers generally are required to withstand the pressure and strain of working in close quarters during busy periods, stand for hours at a time, lift heavy pots and kettles, and work near hot ovens and ranges. Job hazards might include falls, cuts, and burns, but injuries are seldom serious.

Work hours in restaurants might include late evening, holiday, and weekend work, while hours in cafeterias in factories, schools, or other institutions may be more regular. Kitchen workers employed by public and private schools may work during the school year only, usually for nine or ten months. Vacation resorts offer seasonal employment.

Employment

Chefs, cooks, and other kitchen workers held 2.6 million jobs in 1986. Short-order and fast food cooks held 591,000 of the jobs, restaurant cooks 520,000, institutional cooks 389,000, bread and pastry bakers 114,000, and other kitchen workers 949,000.

Nearly two-thirds of all chefs, cooks, and other kitchen workers worked in restaurants and other retail food service establishments.

One-fifth worked in institutions such as schools, universities, prisons, hospitals, and nursing homes. The remainder were employed by hotels, government and factory cafeterias, private clubs, and many other organizations. More than one-third worked part time.

Training

Most kitchen workers start as fast food or short-order cooks or in one of the other less-skilled kitchen positions that require little education or training and that allow them to acquire their skills on the job. After gaining some basic food-handling, preparation, and cooking skills, they might be able to advance to an assistant or fry cook.

Many years of training and experience are necessary, however, to achieve the level of skill required of an executive chef or cook in a fine restaurant. Even though a high school diploma is not required for beginning jobs, it is highly recommended for those planning a career as a cook or chef. High school or vocational school courses in business, arithmetic, and business administration are particularly helpful.

An ever-increasing number of chefs and cooks are obtaining their training through high school or post-high school vocational programs and two- or four-year colleges. Chefs and cooks might also be trained in apprenticeship programs offered by professional culinary institutes, industry associations, and trade unions. An example is the three-year apprenticeship program administered by local chapters of the American Culinary Federation in cooperation with local employees and junior colleges or vocational education institutions. In addition, some large hotels and restaurants operate their own training programs for new employees.

Persons who have had courses in commercial food preparation may be able to start in a cook or chef job without having to spend time in a lower-skilled kitchen job, and they may have an advantage when looking for jobs in better restaurants and hotels, where hiring standards often are high. Some high school vocational programs offer this kind of training. But usually these courses, which range from a few months to two years or more and are open in some cases only to high school graduates, are given by trade schools, vocational centers, colleges, professional associations, and trade unions. The armed forces also are a good source of training and experience.

Curricula vary, but students usually learn to prepare food through actual practice such as broiling, baking, and otherwise preparing food. They also learn to use and care for kitchen equipment. Training programs often include instruction in menu planning, determination of portion size and food cost control, purchasing food supplies in quantity, selecting and storing food, and using leftover food to minimize waste. Students also learn hotel and restaurant sanitation and public health rules regarding food handling.

Training in supervisory and management skills sometimes is emphasized in courses offered by private vocational schools, professional associations, and university programs.

Many school districts, in cooperation with school services divisions of state departments of education, provide on-the-job training and sometimes summer workshops for cafeteria kitchen workers who wish to become cooks. Junior colleges, community colleges, and culinary schools also offer training programs. (See appendix A.)

Certification provides valuable formal recognition of the skills of a chef or cook. The American Culinary Federation certifies chefs and cooks at the levels of cook, chef, pastry chef, executive chef, and master chef. Certification standards are based primarily on experience and formal training.

Other Qualifications

The ability to work as part of a team, a keen sense of taste and smell, and personal cleanliness are important qualifications for chefs, cooks, and other kitchen workers. Most states require health certificates indicating that these workers are free from contagious diseases.

Advancement

Advancement opportunities for chefs and cooks are better than for most other food and beverage preparation and service occupations. Many acquire higher paying positions and new cooking skills by moving from one job to another. Others gradually advance to executive chef positions, particularly in hotels, clubs, or larger, more elegant restaurants.

Some chefs and cooks eventually go into business as caterers or restaurant owners; others might become instructors in vocational programs in high schools, junior and community colleges, and other academic institutions.

Job Outlook

Employment openings for chefs, cooks, and other kitchen workers are expected to be plentiful through the year 2000. Employment growth will create many job openings, but most openings will arise from the need to replace the relatively high proportion of workers who leave this very large occupation each year.

There is substantial turnover in many of these jobs because the limited formal education and training requirements allow easy entry, and the large number of part-time positions are attractive to persons seeking a short-term source of income rather than a career. Many of the workers who leave these jobs transfer to other occupations, while others stop working to assume household responsibilities or to attend school full time.

Workers under the age of twenty-five have traditionally filled a significant proportion of these jobs. The pool of young workers is expected to shrink through the year 2000, however, forcing many employers to offer higher wages, better fringe benefits, and more training to attract and retain workers.

Employment of chefs, cooks, and other kitchen workers is expected to increase faster than the average for all occupations through the year 2000. Because the overall level of economic activity affects restaurant food and beverage sales, sales and employment will increase with the growth of the economy.

Other factors contributing to employment growth will be population growth, rising family and personal incomes, and more leisure time that will allow people to dine out and take vacations more often. Also, as more women join the work force, families increasingly may find dining out a welcome convenience.

Employment in restaurants is expected to grow rapidly. Increasing demand for restaurants that offer table service and varied menus, particularly more expensive restaurants that offer more exotic foods, will require highly skilled cooks and chefs.

Employment in cafeterias in educational services is expected to increase slowly due to the anticipated slow growth of that sector. However, growth of the number of elderly people is expected to result in a rapid increase in kitchen jobs associated with nursing homes, residential care facilities, and other health care institutions.

Earnings

According to a survey conducted by the National Restaurant Association, median hourly earnings of chefs were $8.35 in 1986 and generally ranged between $7.25 and $9.00. Cooks had median hourly earnings of $5.25, with most earning between $4.50 and $6.25. Assistant cooks had median hourly earnings of $4.75, with most earning between $4.00 and $5.00.

According to the same survey, short-order cooks had median hourly earnings of $4.50 in 1986; most earned between $4.00 and $5.00. Median hourly earnings of bread and pastry bakers were $5.04; most earned within the range of $4.94 to $6.00. Salad preparation workers generally earned less, with median hourly earnings of $4.25; most earned between $4.00 and $4.83. Food preparation workers in fast food restaurants had median hourly earnings of $3.85, with most earning between $3.35, the minimum wage, and $4.50.

Wages of chefs, cooks, and other kitchen workers vary depending on the part of the country and especially the type of establishment in which they work. Wages generally are highest in elegant restaurants and hotels. Some employers provide uniforms and free meals, but federal law permits employers to deduct from wages the cost, or fair value, of any meals or lodging provided, and some employers exercise this right.

Executive chefs are responsible for the operation of the kitchen. (Hilton International photo)

CHAPTER 4

MANAGEMENT POSITIONS

There are many different kinds of management positions available in the restaurant industry. Some positions are concerned with certain task activities. These might include the following:

- personnel manager—supervises effective employment orientation, training, and management of employees.
- purchasing manager—maintains profitability of units by controlling costs, authorizing expenditures, and reviewing results.
- operations manager—enforces consistent company standards, systems, and procedures.
- marketing and promotions manager—implements store marketing concepts, programs, and advertising campaigns.
- finance manager—monitors performance, prepares budgets, and develops sales forecasts.

Other restaurants are set up in such a way that managers oversee certain sections of the restaurant or are in charge at specific times. The list includes:

- kitchen
- dining room
- night

- regional
- district
- unit
- assistant unit

In restaurants, the manager is assisted by one or more assistant managers, depending on the size and business hours of the establishment. In large establishments as well as many others that offer fine dining, the management team consists of a general manager, one or more assistant managers, and an executive chef. The executive chef is responsible for the operation of the kitchen, while the assistant managers oversee service in the dining room and other areas of the operation. However, in smaller establishments, the executive chef may also be the general manager and sometimes the owner.

Obviously, managers of small operations perform more varied tasks, while managers in larger establishments have more specialized responsibilities.

NATURE OF THE WORK

The efficient and profitable operation of restaurants requires that managers select and appropriately price interesting menu items; make efficient use of food, beverages, and other supplies; achieve consistent quality in food preparation and service; recruit and train adequate numbers of workers; and painstakingly attend to the various administrative aspects of the business.

Managers or executive chefs select menu items, taking into account the likely number of customers, the past popularity of various dishes, and considerations such as food left over from meals that should not be wasted, the need for variety on the menu, and the availability of foods due to seasonal and other factors.

Managers analyze the recipes of the dishes to determine food, labor, and overhead costs and assign prices to the menu items. Menus must be developed far enough in advance to receive needed supplies in time.

On a daily basis, managers estimate food consumption, place orders with suppliers, and schedule the delivery of fresh food and beverages. They receive and check the content of deliveries, evaluating the quality of meats, poultry, fish, fruits, vegetables, and baked goods.

Managers meet and talk with sales representatives of restaurant suppliers to place orders to replenish stocks of tableware, linens, paper, cleaning supplies, cooking utensils, and furniture and fixtures. They also arrange for equipment repairs.

Managers interview, hire, and, when necessary, discharge workers. They familiarize newly hired workers with the establishment's policies and practices and oversee their training. Managers schedule the work hours of employees, ensuring that there are adequate numbers of workers present during busy periods but not too many during slow periods.

Managers supervise the preparation of food in the kitchen and the serving of meals in the dining room. They oversee food preparation and cooking, checking the quality of the food and the sizes of portions to ensure that dishes are prepared and garnished correctly and in a timely manner.

If customers complain about service or food quality, it is the manager's job to investigate and resolve the issue.

During busy periods, managers often have to roll up their sleeves and help with the cooking, cleaning of tables, or other tasks.

Managers direct the cleaning of the kitchen and dining areas and the washing of tableware, kitchen utensils, and equipment to maintain company and government sanitation standards.

Managers monitor workers and observe patrons on a continual basis to make sure that health and safety standards as well as local liquor regulations are complied with.

Managers also have a variety of administrative responsibilities. In larger establishments, much of this work is done by a bookkeeper, but in others, managers are responsible for keeping accurate records of the hours and wages of employees, preparing the payroll, and doing paperwork to comply with licensing laws and reporting requirements of tax, wage and hour, unemployment compensation, and Social Security laws. They also must maintain records of the costs of supplies and equipment purchased and ensure that accounts with suppliers are paid on a regular basis.

In addition, managers record the number, type, and cost of items sold to weed out dishes that are unpopular or less profitable. Many managers now use computers to help ease the burden of paperwork.

At the end of each day or sometimes each shift, managers must tally the cash and credit card receipts and balance them against the records of sales. They are responsible for depositing the day's income at the bank or securing it in a safe place. Managers are also responsible for locking the doors and making sure that ovens, grills, and lights are off and alarm systems are switched on.

WORKING CONDITIONS

Managers are the first to arrive and the last to leave at night. Because evenings and weekends are popular dining periods, night and weekend work is common. Many restaurant managers work sixty hours or more each week. More conventional hours are worked by those managers in institutional food service facilities because factory and office cafeterias are open only on weekdays for breakfast and lunch.

Restaurant managers sometimes experience the pressures of coordinating a wide range of functions. The job can be hectic during peak dining hours, and dealing with irate customers or uncooperative employees can be particularly stressful. However, the working conditions are usually clean, well lighted, and air conditioned.

EMPLOYMENT

Restaurant managers held about 470,000 jobs in 1986. Most worked in eating and drinking establishments, but small numbers also were employed by educational institutions, hospitals, nursing and personal care facilities, department stores, and civic, social, and fraternal organizations.

Nearly half were self-employed. Jobs are located throughout the country but are most plentiful in large cities and tourist areas.

TRAINING

Many restaurant management positions are filled by promoting experienced food and beverage preparation and service workers. Waiters, waitresses, chefs, and fast food workers who have demonstrated their potential for handling increased responsibilities sometimes advance to assistant manager or management-trainee jobs when openings occur.

Just as executive chefs need extensive experience working as a chef, general managers need experience working as an assistant. However, most food service management companies and national or regional chains also recruit management trainees from among the graduates of two-year and four-year college programs.

Food service and restaurant chains prefer to hire persons with degrees in restaurant and institutional food service management, but they often hire graduates with degrees in other fields who have demonstrated interest and aptitude.

A bachelor's degree in restaurant and food service management provides a particularly strong preparation for a career in this occupation. In 1986, more than 130 colleges and universities offered four-year programs in restaurant and hotel management or institutional food service management.

For persons who do not want to pursue a four-year degree, a good alternative background is provided by the more than two hundred community and junior colleges, technical institutes, and other institutions that offer programs in these fields leading to an associate degree or other formal award below the baccalaureate.

Both two-year and four-year programs provide instruction in subjects such as accounting, business law and management, food planning and preparation, and nutrition. Some programs combine classroom and laboratory study with internships that provide on-the-job experience.

In addition, more than one hundred educational institutions offer culinary programs that provide food preparation training which can lead to a career as a cook or chef and provide a foundation for advancement to an executive chef position.

OTHER QUALIFICATIONS

Perhaps as in no other industry, the emphasis for restaurant employees is on personal qualities. The right personality is a crucial factor. Restaurant managers must genuinely like and understand people. To the restaurant staff, they must be fair and respected for their leadership. To customers, they must appear hardworking, sympathetic, and capable of dealing with almost any situation or demand, often under pressure.

Because restaurant management can be so demanding, good health and stamina are important attributes for a manager to have. Self-discipline, initiative, and leadership ability are essential. Managers must be able to make decisions, solve problems, and concentrate on details. Good communication skills are necessary to deal with customers and suppliers as well as to direct subordinates. A neat and clean appearance is required, and a sense of humor is an asset.

Most companies offer extensive management-trainee programs. Through a combination of classroom and on-the-job training, trainees receive instruction and gain work experience in all aspects of restaurant operation including food preparation, sanitation, security, company policies and procedures, personnel management, record keeping, and preparation of reports. Usually after six months or a year, trainees receive their first permanent assignment as an assistant manager.

ADVANCEMENT

Willingness to relocate often is essential for advancement to positions with greater responsibility. Managers advance to larger establishments or regional management positions with restaurant chains. Some managers eventually open their own restaurants. Others are able to transfer to hotel management positions because their experience is a good background for food and beverage director jobs at hotels and resorts.

JOB OUTLOOK

Employment of restaurant managers is expected to increase faster than the average for all occupations through the year 2000. In addition to growth in demand for these managers, the need to replace managers who transfer to other occupations or stop working for a variety of reasons will create many new jobs. Opportunities are expected to be best for persons with bachelor's or associate degrees in restaurant institutional food service management.

Employment will increase with growth in the number of eating and drinking establishments. Population growth, rising personal incomes, increased leisure time, and more two-income families are factors that will continue to add to the number of meals consumed outside the home.

Employment of managers in school and college cafeterias is expected to increase relatively slowly due to the anticipated slow growth in total student enrollments. However, growth in the number of elderly people is expected to create rapid growth of food service management positions in nursing homes, residential care facilities, and other health care institutions.

EARNINGS

According to the type and size of establishment, earnings of restaurant and food service managers vary greatly. Based on a survey conducted for the National Restaurant Association, the median base salary was estimated to be $22,400 a year in 1986. However, managers of the largest restaurants and institutional food service facilities often had annual salaries in excess of $40,000.

Fast food restaurant managers had an estimated median base salary of $15,700 a year; managers of full-menu restaurants with table service, $22,000; and managers of commercial and institutional cafeterias, $25,400 a year in 1986.

In addition to a salary, most managers received an annual bonus or incentive payment based on their performance. In 1986, most of these payments ranged between $3,000 and $7,500 a year.

Executive chefs had an estimated median base salary of $22,700 a year in 1986, but those employed in the largest food service facilities often had base salaries over $35,000. Annual bonus or incentive payments of most executive chefs ranged between $1,500 and $7,000 a year.

The median base salary of assistant managers was $18,900 a year in 1986 but ranged from $13,100 in fast food restaurants to over $28,700 in some of the largest restaurants and food service facilities. Annual bonus or incentive payments ranged between $1,000 and $3,000 a year.

Manager trainees had a median base salary of $13,100 a year in 1986 but had salaries of more than $20,000 in some of the largest food service facilities, with bonuses ranging from between $600 and $1,600 a year.

Most restaurant and food service managers received free meals, sick leave, health and accident insurance, and one to three weeks of paid vacation a year, depending on length of service.

A food and beverage director confers with the managers of the kitchen and dining room staffs. (Hyatt Regency photo)

CHAPTER 5

FOOD AND BEVERAGE DIRECTORS

Food and beverage directors are responsible for the overall operation and coordination of all food and beverage departments in hotels, motels, and some fine restaurants that have large staffs. As mentioned previously, many food service jobs overlap one another. The smaller the operation, the more hats each employee wears; the larger the establishment, the more specialized the jobs become. But food and beverage directors oversee all of these specialized jobs.

NATURE OF THE JOB

Food and beverage directors oversee the work of the purchasing, kitchen, and dining room staffs. They must possess a thorough knowledge of all the jobs the workers on these staffs perform because they are responsible for selecting, training, and motivating each staff member.

The purchasing staff buys food for the chef and kitchen staff to prepare. The dining room staff serves the guests. A major responsibility of food and beverage directors is to coordinate the efforts of the three staffs from start to finish. And they must do it in a way that maintains and improves productivity, food quality, service, creativity, and merchandising in order to increase volume, sales, and profits.

To provide the best possible service to guests, food and beverage directors must keep other operating departments informed concerning the activities of the food and beverage department. They must ensure that the decisions made correspond to those of the general manager and the approved policies of the establishment.

When necessary, food and beverage directors recommend changes or innovations in policy, procedure, or equipment to the management staff.

Food and beverage directors schedule the times of operation of all restaurants and bars to achieve the most profitable result. They establish purchasing and receiving procedures and ensure that all the supplies ordered are received in the quantities requested as well as in proper condition.

Food and beverage directors assess and analyze competitors; they review prices, sources of supply, food and beverage trends, and inventories. And they hire and discharge workers.

WORKING CONDITIONS

Food and beverage directors are involved in administrative work so they usually have their own private offices. However, their responsibilities take them to all parts of the restaurant, and they are on their feet a good part of the day. Although they are usually scheduled to work about forty hours a week, many times they must work more than that. Their hours may be irregular because they supervise workers in various shifts. They sometimes experience the pressures of coordinating a wide range of functions. In hotels, conventions and large groups of tourists can cause additional stress for food and beverage directors.

EMPLOYMENT

Because each hotel has only one food and beverage director, the competition can be keen. Jobs are located throughout the country but are most plentiful in large cities and tourist areas.

TRAINING

Postsecondary training in hotel or restaurant management is preferred for most food and beverage director positions, although a college liberal arts degree may be sufficient when coupled with related hotel experience.

In the past, most food and beverage directors were promoted from the ranks of lower positions within the establishment. And while some persons can still become food and beverage directors without benefit of education beyond high school, it is becoming more and more difficult.

Specialized hotel experience is an asset to all persons seeking food and beverage management careers. And in many hotel chains, specialized hotel or restaurant training is preferred or even required. Because a hotel's restaurant and cocktail lounge are often of great importance to the success of the entire establishment, restaurant management training or experience is an acceptable background for entering hotel management.

A bachelor's degree in hotel and restaurant administration provides particularly strong preparation for a career as a food and beverage director.

In 1986, more than one hundred colleges and universities offered four-year programs in hotel management. More than two hundred community and junior colleges, technical institutes, and vocational and trade schools and other academic institutions also have programs leading to an associate degree or other formal recognition in hotel or restaurant management. (See appendix A.)

Graduates of hotel or restaurant management programs are able to start as trainee assistant managers or at least to advance to such positions more quickly.

OTHER QUALIFICATIONS

Food and beverage directors must be able to get along with all kinds of people, even in the most stressful situations. They need initiative, self-discipline, and the ability to organize and direct the work of others. They must have the ability to solve problems and concentrate on details. Some hotels insist that food and beverage directors speak one or two additional languages besides English.

ADVANCEMENT

Most hotels promote employees who have proven their ability. Newly built hotels, particularly those without well-established, on-the-job training programs, often prefer experienced personnel for managerial positions.

Large hotels and motel chains may offer better opportunities for advancement than small, independently owned establishments, but frequent relocation is often necessary. Large chains can offer more extensive career ladder programs where food and beverage directors are offered the opportunity to transfer to another hotel or motel in the chain or to the central office if an opening occurs.

JOB OUTLOOK

Employment of food and beverage directors is expected to grow faster than the average for all occupations through the year 2000 as more large hotels, motels, and restaurant chains are built. Business travel will continue to grow, and increased domestic and foreign tourism will also create demand for additional hotels and motels. Most openings are expected to occur as experienced food and beverage directors transfer, retire, or stop working.

EARNINGS

In 1986, food and beverage directors averaged an estimated $42,000 a year, based on a survey conducted for the American Hotel and Motel Association. In addition, food and beverage directors may earn bonuses ranging up to 20 percent of their base salary in some establishments. They and their families may also be furnished with lodging, meals, parking, laundry, and other services.

Most food and beverage directors receive five to ten paid holidays a year, paid vacation, sick leave, life insurance, medical benefits, and pension plans. Some hotels offer profit-sharing plans, educational assistance, and other benefits to their employees.

CHAPTER 6

CERTIFIED MASTER CHEF: THE HIGHEST HONOR IN THE INDUSTRY

There are thirty-eight certified master chefs (CMCs) in the United States. This designation, acknowledged worldwide, represents the highest recognition a professional chef can attain. Europe, which has been implementing the master certification program for more than half a century, has thousands of certified master chefs. But the title and the distinction is a new one in the United States. It was offered for the first time in 1981.

The thirty-eight CMCs are highly trained individuals who are deeply dedicated to their profession.

THE MASTER CHEF CERTIFICATION PROGRAM

Master chef certification (MCC) results from the most rigorous testing a professional chef can encounter. Ferdinand Metz, president of the Culinary Institute of America in Hyde Park, New York, was instrumental in developing the MCC program.

When I was charged with the task of developing an MCC program, I went to very logical sources—primarily my brother and my father who are both Certified Master Chefs in Europe. From them, my training in Europe and my travels, I was able to compile a comprehensive program.

The program in the United States had to be more stringent and more comprehensive than its foreign counterparts, because America is comprised of a combination of almost every nation; whereas in Europe most chefs focus on classical cuisine with a bit of regional cooking. It was my intention to establish a program that would have integrity and would be mutually recognized under the reciprocal arrangement with any nation in Europe. That was achieved.

Each candidate for master chef certification is a certified executive chef with many years of experience in the world of food. Candidates for MCC enroll in the American Culinary Federation's intensive ten-day program held at the Culinary Institute of America in New York. They must complete the required course load, which includes the following topics:

- American cuisine
- international cuisine
- classical cuisine
- bakery/pastry/patisserie
- dietary cooking/nutrition
- tableside cooking
- cold buffet preparation
- food science
- menu development
- managerial development
- beverage control and service
- dining room service and supervision

Once the course load is completed, all candidates are required to pass theoretical and practical examinations.

Chefs spend a great deal of time studying for these examinations. Some CMCs have reported spending six months in intensive preparation, studying sixteen hours a day. In addition to their time, chefs invest about $2,000 in tuition, fees, materials, and living expenses.

PASSING THE EXAM

After a lifetime of preparation and months of intensive study, the chefs undergo examinations that begin at 7 A.M. and end at 9 P.M. Candidates are required to perform under the constant, watchful eye of judges and students. Obviously, chefs must be in top mental and physical shape to begin a testing program of this intensity.

Food must be prepared at the exact time specified—not five minutes before or five minutes after. This pressure causes burnout for some candidates who depart before the program's completion. The success rate has been a discouragingly low 45 percent.

Chefs who have successfully completed the program, however, support its structure. One CMC explained it this way: "The testing has to be as tough and intensive as it is, because a chef must work well under pressure. If you can't, then you're not a master."

THE BENEFITS OF BECOMING A CMC

One might wonder why successful, well-respected professionals would subject themselves to this kind of rigorous testing. The certified master chefs said the challenge of the program was a very appealing factor. But the motivating factor is that they want to advance the profession as well as set an example for student chefs and peers.

Aside from the great honor attached to being classified as the best, master chef certification also includes privileges, rewards, and responsibilities.

The privileges include being recognized as a top professional in the culinary field, assuming a professional leadership role, and upgrading culinary standards.

More tangible rewards include job offers, raises, promotions, and publicity. Master chef certification brings status to the CMC's establishment and provides inspiration to others wishing to attain the same distinction.

Along with the title come responsibilities. Once granted master chef certification, chefs administer future examinations to guarantee quality control. Other responsibilities include:

- maintaining and upgrading the high standards of the culinary arts
- representing the profession outside the industry
- supporting the American Culinary Foundation (ACF) by lecturing, teaching ACF apprentices, and serving as judges for national and international competitions

After becoming a CMC and receiving the highest honor the profession can bestow, certified master chefs still have a challenge. It is to live up to their reputations, to continue learning, and to pass their knowledge on to other chefs.

WHAT THE CMC PROGRAM MEANS TO THE RESTAURANT INDUSTRY

Certified master chef Ferdinand Metz summed up the program's value to the restaurant industry in this way:

> When I came to this country in 1962, anybody could put on a white hat and claim to be a chef. No one could dispute it. Foodservice at that time was in sad, sad shape. Today it has improved tremendously. Almost 100 percent of the thousands of students CIA graduates every year have Master Chef Certification as their ultimate goal. When they achieve this goal, it will tell them something about themselves, and it will also tell the outside world about them. Becoming a CMC is a culmination of many years of experience, which add up to quality, expertise, professionalism and recognition.
>
> The Master Chef Certification program is still in its infancy in the United States. Relatively few people outside of the industry have ever heard of it. Once it becomes more widely known—and it will be—the public will render the title of Certified Master Chef its just respect and admiration. When that happens, the entire foodservice industry will benefit.

There are numerous opportunities in the restaurant industry, as about 175,000 new employees will be needed each year to keep pace with demand. (School of Hotel Administration photo)

CHAPTER 7

TOP EXECUTIVES IN THE RESTAURANT INDUSTRY

The restaurant industry is distinct in that the owner of a single-unit, twenty-seat diner, who may have to wash dishes and sweep the floor, is also the establishment's chief executive officer. This owner would be the chairman of the board—if there were a board of directors. And although the owner may have only one employee, he or she is the president.

As the top executive, a single-unit owner is responsible for making the decisions on how to run the business. He or she owns the establishment, and that says it all.

Although one-unit owners may have a common bond with the owners of very large, international chains such as McDonald's or Burger King, their average workdays and their average salaries are very different.

In this chapter, the focus is on those restaurant establishments large enough to require top executives to oversee the managers. These individuals have reached the top of the management ladder and are sometimes called general managers or executive vice-presidents.

General managers and executive vice-presidents are responsible for planning, organizing, directing, controlling, and coordinating the operations of an organization and its major departments or programs. The members of the board of directors and supervisory managers are also involved in these activities.

Individual departments that general managers and executive vice-presidents oversee include the following:

- operations
- finance
- marketing
- advertising
- human relations
- distribution/purchasing
- recruitment
- training

NATURE OF THE WORK

The fundamental objective of any business venture, including all types of restaurant establishments, is to maintain efficiency and profitability in the face of accelerating technological complexity and acute and ever-increasing competition.

A large restaurant corporation's general goals and policies are established by the chief executive officer in collaboration with other top executives, usually executive vice-presidents, and with a board of directors. Often, busy chief executive officers meet with top executives of other similar restaurant establishments to discuss matters affecting the industry. Although the chief executive officer retains ultimate authority and responsibility, the chief operating officer may be delegated the authority to oversee executive vice-presidents who direct the activities of various departments and are responsible for carrying out the organization's goals.

The responsibilities of executive vice-presidents depend greatly upon the size of the restaurant establishment. In large corporations, their duties may be highly specialized. For example, they may oversee the activities of general managers of marketing, sales promotion, purchasing, finance, personnel, training, administrative service, property management, or legal services. In smaller establishments, an executive vice-president might be responsible for a number of these departments.

General managers, in turn, direct their individual department's activities within the framework of the organization's overall plan. With the help of supervisory managers and their staffs, general managers strive to achieve the department's goals as rapidly and economically as possible.

WORKING CONDITIONS

It is not unusual for top executives to be provided with spacious, lavish offices, and many enjoy numerous benefits. General managers are provided with comfortable offices close to the departments they direct and to the executive vice-presidents to whom they report. Long hours, including evenings and weekends, are the rule, and business discussions might occupy most of their time during social engagements.

Substantial travel is often required. General managers may have to travel between national, regional, and local offices. Executive vice-presidents may travel to meet with their counterparts in other corporations in the country, or even overseas. Meetings and conferences sponsored by industries and associations occur regularly and provide invaluable opportunities to meet with peers and keep abreast of technological and other developments. A prime example of this is the National Restaurant Association's annual show, which occurs every spring.

In large corporations, job transfers between the parent company and its local offices or subsidiaries, here or abroad, are common.

General managers and top executives of restaurant operations very often work under intense pressure to attain their goals. And sometimes they find themselves in situations over which they have limited influence, for example, when meeting with government officials, private interest groups, or competitors.

EMPLOYMENT

General managers and top executives held about 2.4 million jobs, although not all in the restaurant industry, in 1986. Although these positions are found in every industry, employment is more concentrated in the largest industries like the restaurant business.

TRAINING

The educational background of managers and top executives varies as widely as the nature of their diverse responsibilities. Most general managers and top executives have a bachelor's degree in liberal arts or business administration. Their academic major is often related to the departments they direct—for example, accounting for a general manager of finance or computer science for a general manager of data processing. Graduate and professional degrees are common. Many managers in administrative, marketing, financial, and manufacturing activities have a master's degree in business administration.

Managers in highly technical manufacturing and research activities, such as food technology, often have a master's or doctoral degree in an engineering or scientific discipline. A law degree is necessary for general managers of corporate legal departments.

In the restaurant industry, as well as in retail trade, competent individuals without a college degree may become general managers. But for most general managers, experience is still the primary qualification.

Most general management and top executive positions are filled by promoting experienced lower-level managers who display the leadership, self-confidence, motivation, decisiveness, and flexibility required by these demanding positions. In small firms, where the number of positions is limited, advancement to a higher management position may come slowly. In large firms, promotions may occur more quickly. It is suggested that those who wish to accelerate the advancement process take advantage of company training programs to broaden their knowledge of company policy and operations.

For example, attendance at seminars sponsored by the National Restaurant Association held throughout the country can familiarize managers with the latest developments in management techniques. Participation in these conferences and seminars can expand their knowledge of national and international issues influencing the restaurant industry.

Persons interested in becoming general managers and top executives must possess highly developed personal skills. A highly analytical mind able to quickly assess large amounts of information and data is very important.

The ability to consider and evaluate the interrelationships of numerous factors and to select the best course of action is imperative. In the absence of sufficient information, sound intuitive managerial judgment is crucial to reaching favorable decisions.

General managers and top executives also must be able to communicate clearly and persuasively, both orally and in writing.

General managers may advance to a top executive position, such as executive or administrative vice-president, in their own establishment or to a corresponding general management position in a larger establishment.

Similarly, top-level managers may advance to peak corporate positions such as chief operating officer and finally chief executive officer. Chief executive officers, upon retirement, may become members of the board of directors of one or more firms. Some general managers and top executives with sufficient capital establish their own restaurant businesses.

JOB OUTLOOK

Employment of general managers and top executives is expected to increase about as fast as the average for all occupations through the year 2000 as businesses grow in number, size, and complexity. However, much-faster-than-average employment growth is projected in the hotel, restaurant, and travel industries as personal income and leisure time increase. In addition to openings arising from increased demand for these managers and executives, many job openings will occur each year to replace those who transfer to better paying positions, start their own businesses, or retire.

However, the ample supply of competent, experienced lower-level managers seeking top management positions should result in substantial job competition. Outstanding individuals whose accomplishments reflect leadership qualities and the ability to improve the efficiency or competitive position of their organization will have the best employment opportunities.

EARNINGS

The estimated median annual salary of general managers and top executives was around $34,000 in 1986. Many earned well over $52,000. Salary levels vary substantially depending upon the level of managerial responsibility; length of service; and type, size, and location of the firm.

Most salaried general managers and top executives in the restaurant industry receive additional compensation in the form of bonuses, stock awards, and cash-equivalent fringe benefits such as company-paid insurance premiums, use of company cars, and paid country club or health club memberships.

Chief executive officers of large corporations are the most highly paid top-level managers. A survey of top publicly held corporations revealed that in 1986, over a hundred chief executive officers received base salaries of $1 million or more with additional compensation, such as fringe benefits and company stock, equivalent, on average, to nearly half of their base salary. Other surveys of executive salaries reveal the importance of the size of the corporation. A top-level manager in a very large corporation can earn ten times as much as a counterpart in a small firm.

Salaries also vary substantially by industry and geographic location. For example, salaries in large metropolitan areas such as New York City are normally higher than those in small cities and towns.

Food scientist-technologists search for ways to retain the characteristics and nutritive value of foods during processing and storage. (Cornell University photo)

CHAPTER 8

BEHIND-THE-SCENE WORKERS

This chapter focuses on positions that have recently become more and more important to the restaurant industry. These positions include dietitians, menu planners, and food scientist-technologists. Often these individuals work in offices or laboratories away from the restaurant operation.

DIETITIANS AND NUTRITIONISTS

Dietitians, sometimes called nutritionists, are professionals trained in applying the principles of nutrition to food selection and meal preparation.

In today's society, there is a growing concern for physical fitness and healthful eating habits. Restaurant operators are aware of this trend, and many are taking steps to alter their menus accordingly. An increasing number of restaurant operators are hiring or, at least, consulting with dietitians and nutritionists when planning their food offerings.

Dietitians and nutritionists perform the following services:

- counsel individuals and groups in the basics of sound nutrition to promote good health
- set up and supervise food service systems for institutions such as hospitals, prisons, schools, and large restaurant chains
- promote sound eating habits through education and research
- analyze the nutritional content of food for labeling purposes or marketing efforts

In addition to restaurants, dietitians may run the food service departments of small hospitals. In this capacity, dietitians are responsible for establishing long-term nutritional care programs and a system of close monitoring of individual patients. When necessary, they must be able to prepare custom-mixed, high-nutrition formulas for patients who require tube or intravenous feedings.

Administrative dietitians are responsible for large-scale meal planning and preparation in such places as hospitals, company cafeterias, prisons, schools, and colleges and universities.

In this capacity, dietitians and nutritionists perform the following tasks:

- supervise the planning, preparation, and serving of meals
- select, train, and direct food service supervisors and workers
- budget for and purchase food, equipment, and supplies
- enforce sanitary and safety regulations
- prepare records and reports

Increasingly, dietitians use computer programs to plan meals that satisfy nutritional requirements and are economical at the same time. Dietitians who are directors of dietetic departments also decide on departmental policy, coordinate dietetic services with the activities of other departments, and develop and maintain the dietetic department budget, which in large organizations may amount to millions of dollars annually.

Research dietitians use established research methods and analytical techniques to conduct studies in areas that range from basic science to practical applications. Research dietitians may examine changes in the way the body uses food over the course of a lifetime, for example, or study the interaction of drugs and diet. They may investigate nutritional needs of persons with particular diseases, behavior modification as it relates to diet and nutrition, or applied topics such as food service systems and equipment.

Often research dietitians are called on to make their findings known to the restaurant industry by preparing research papers and oral presentations.

Working Conditions

Most dietitians work forty hours a week. Those who are employed in hospitals sometimes work on weekends, while those in commercial food services tend to have irregular hours.

Dietitians and nutritionists spend much of their time in clean, well-lighted, and well-ventilated areas such as research laboratories, classrooms, or offices near food preparation areas. However, they may spend time in kitchens and serving areas that are often hot and steamy and where some light lifting may be required. Dietitians and nutritionists may be on their feet for most of the workday. Those who are involved in consulting spend a significant amount of time traveling.

Employment

Dietitians and nutritionists held about forty thousand jobs in 1986. Hospitals and nursing homes are a major source of employment for dietitions and nutritionists, accounting for just over half of all jobs in this field in 1986. Firms that provide food services for hospital patients on a contract basis employ a small but growing number of dietitians and nutritionists.

Local government programs and schools, colleges, and universities provide over 15 percent of dietitian jobs. Other jobs for dietitians and nutritionists are found in prison systems, hotel and restaurant chains, and companies that provide food service for their employees.

Many dietitians and nutritionists work as consultants, either full time or part time. In addition to serving on the staff of a hospital, for example, a dietitian may be a consultant for another health care facility. Nursing homes use consultants or part-time workers to provide much of their dietetic supervision.

Training

The basic requirement for this field is a bachelor's degree with a major in foods and nutrition or institution management. This degree can be earned in about 270 colleges and universities, usually in departments of home economics or food and nutrition sciences. In addition to basic educational requirements, required college courses include foods, nutrition, institution management, chemistry, microbiology, and physiology. Other important courses are mathematics, statistics, computer science, psychology, sociology, and economics.

To qualify for professional credentials as a registered dietitian, the American Dietetic Association recommends one of the following educational paths:

- completion of a four-year coordinated undergraduate program which includes nine hundred to one thousand hours of clinical experience
- completion of a bachelor's degree from an approved program plus an accredited dietetic internship
- completion of a bachelor's or master's degree from an approved program and six months' approved work experience

Internships last six to twelve months and combine clinical experience under a qualified dietitian with some classroom work. In 1987, 103 internship programs were accredited by the American Dietetic Association. Coordinated undergraduate programs enable students to complete their clinical experience requirement while obtaining their bachelor's degree. In 1987, sixty-five such programs were offered in colleges and universities. These programs are accredited by the American Dietetic Association.

Other Qualifications

Persons who are planning to become dietitians or nutritionists should have organizational and administrative ability as well as scientific aptitude. They should also be able to work well with people.

Among the courses recommended for high school students interested in careers as dietitians are home economics, business, biology, health, mathematics, communications, and chemistry. Computer courses are valuable because dietitians and nutritionists use them for planning meals, keeping inventory, and analyzing the nutritional content of proposed diets.

Advancement

Experienced dietitians and nutritioninsts may advance to assistant or associate director or director of a dietetic department. Advancement to higher level positions in teaching and research requires graduate education; public health nutritionists usually must earn a graduate degree. Graduate study in institutional or business administration is valuable to those interested in administrative dietetics.

Clinical specialization offers another path to career advancement. Specialty areas for clinical dietitians include kidney disease, diabetes, cancer, heart disease, pediatrics, and gerontology.

Job Outlook

Employment of dietitians and nutritionists is expected to grow faster than the average for all occupations through the year 2000 to meet the expanding need for individual and group meals in nursing homes, hospitals, retirement and life-care communities, and social service programs of various kinds.

Most job openings, however, will result from the need to replace experienced workers who stop working or change occupations. A number of experienced dietitians and nutritionists are moving into management positions in private industry, including food service establishments.

The factors that underlie anticipated rapid expansion of the health services industry—population growth and aging, emphasis on health education, and promotion of prudent life styles and eating habits, as well as widespread ability to pay for care through public and private health insurance—will increase the demand for dietitians and nutritionists.

Demand is also expected to grow in commercial settings, including catering firms, restaurant chains, and medical supply firms. In addition, dietitians and nutritionists will be needed to staff community health programs to provide nutritional counseling for employer-sponsored wellness and fitness programs and to conduct research in food and nutrition.

Staffing flexibility can be facilitated by using full-time and part-time staff. For this reason, opportunities for part-time employment should remain favorable. This will be especially true in nursing homes, where dietetic services are frequently provided for only a few hours each week.

Opportunities will be best for individuals with experience and for those willing to relocate to areas of greatest demand.

Earnings

Entry-level salaries of dietitians in hospitals averaged $20,400 a year in 1986, according to a national survey conducted by the University of Texas medical branch. The maximum salaries for dietitians in hospitals averaged about $26,600 a year. Salaries may vary by region.

Dietitians and nutritionists usually receive benefits such as paid vacations, sick leave, holidays, health insurance, and retirement benefits.

MENU PLANNERS

The menu planner's work is similar to the work of dietitians and nutritionists. However, it is not quite so technical and doesn't require the same amount of education.

Nature of the Work

Menu planners do exactly what their title implies; they decide what dishes are to be offered to restaurant or institutional patrons.

They are charged with planning menus that are nutritionally balanced, pleasing to the eye, and possible to prepare in large quantities. Menu planners must keep many factors in mind while doing their job, specifically taste, color, nutrition, and cost.

Because restaurant patrons are constantly seeking the new and exciting side of food, menu planners are continually revising menus, developing new recipes, and introducing new dishes to please the customers.

Menu planners work with cooks, chefs, and other dining room and kitchen workers to ask advice, make suggestions, and solve technical problems. At times, the executive chef supervises their work.

A constant challenge for menu planners in large institutional cafeterias is to put variety into their menus. They meet this challenge by ordering unusual ingredients and discovering new recipes.

Menu planners who work in national chain restaurants try to standardize recipes so that a bowl of onion soup in San Francisco tastes the same as one in Minneapolis. Menu planners who are employed by franchise companies are also concerned with trying to make food produced in very large quantities look and taste as though it were prepared individually.

In addition to restaurants, menu planners are employed in hotels, hospitals, schools and universities, prisons, airlines, cafeterias, and other large dining facilities.

Working Conditions

Generally, menu planners enjoy very pleasant working conditions. They spend most of their time sitting at a desk in clean, well-lit offices conveniently located near the kitchen. Their jobs are much less stressful than other restaurant employees because they work behind the scenes and are not subject to demands of evening, holiday, or weekend crowds.

Employment

Menu planners usually work in large restaurants, hotels, hospitals, prisons, airlines, schools and universities, and cafeterias.

Training

Often individual college course work in dietetics or nutrition is enough to qualify for the position of menu planner. However, a bachelor's degree in one of these fields is sometimes required and never wasted. Some chain restaurants and large hotels offer on-the-job training as well.

Would-be menu planners can find excellent courses—including food technology, recipe development, and quantity food production—at vocational schools.

Other Qualifications

Menu planners must have the ability to imagine how food will look on the customer's plate. A good sense of taste and smell is also necessary. And as with any job in the restaurant industry, a menu planner must work well with people.

Advancement

Menu planners can advance to food and beverage managers, catering managers, or directors of all dining facilities. Advancement opportunities are greatest in large hotels, restaurants, and institutions.

Job Outlook

Employment of menu planners is expected to grow faster than the average for all occupations through the year 2000 to meet the expanding need for such services.

Most job openings, however, will result from the need to replace experienced workers who stop working or change occupations. A number of experienced menu planners move into management positions. Menu planners who have a strong background in dietetics may want to work in the food production industry.

Opportunities will be best for individuals with experience and for those willing to relocate to areas of greatest demand.

Earnings

The average salary for menu planners trained in vocational schools was about $16,000 to $19,000 in the mid-1980s. Salaries may vary by region.

Menu planners usually receive benefits such as free meals, paid vacations, sick leave, holidays, health insurance, and pension plans.

FOOD SCIENTIST-TECHNOLOGISTS

As our world becomes more and more sophisticated, new and more technical jobs are created. For example, to meet the food requirements of men and women in today's changing environment, food scientist-technologists are necessary.

According to experts at the Institute of Food Technologists in Chicago, the need for food research is creating a steady demand for persons trained as food scientist-technologists. And according to Professor William Marion, head of the Food Technology Department at Iowa State University, the field is becoming more precisely defined in light of new research findings. "In the past, the food scientist-technologist was simply called a food technologist," he said. "Within that broad heading, he or she performed a number of scientific and technical tasks. Today, this person is now called a food scientist-technologist."

Nature of Job

A food scientist-technologist, depending on the company or organization he or she is working for, may function as a scientist or technologist or both. But Marion maintains that it is important to draw the line between the two sets of responsibilities. "Generally speaking, the food scientist is concerned with the fundamental properties of food, taking into effect color, nutritive value and caloric content. If you were working as a technologist, you would be involved with product development, processing and quality control."

Working Conditions

Approximately one-third of all food scientist-technologists work in research and development, while others work in quality assurance laboratories in production or processing areas of food plants. A small number teach or do basic research in colleges and universities. Others hold sales and management positions.

Food scientist-technologists search for ways to retain the characteristics and nutritive value of foods during processing and storage. They also supervise chemical and microbiological tests to see that products meet industry and government requirements. Processed foods, for example, must be tested for:

- sugar
- starch
- protein
- fat
- vitamin
- mineral content

Food scientist-technologists work in quality control laboratories, where they study raw ingredients for freshness, maturity, and suitability for processing. On a regular basis, they inspect processing line operations to ensure conformance with government and industry standards. Food scientist-technologists must be sure that after processing, various enzymes are inactive and bacterial levels are low enough so that food will not spoil or present a safety hazard.

Food scientist-technologists who work in processing plants have a number of different responsibilities, which include the following:

- preparing production specifications
- scheduling processing operations
- maintaining proper temperature and humidity in storage areas
- supervising sanitation operations, including the proper disposal of wastes
- advising management concerning the purchase of equipment and supplies to increase efficiency

Training

Food scientist-technologists should have a bachelor's degree in food technology. There are about forty universities around the country offering programs in food technology. For students who want to break into the industry gradually, junior and community colleges offer associate certificates in the food processing area.

Earnings

Salaries within the food scientist-technologist field vary with educational background and the type of organization. Large companies generally pay better than government agencies and universities. Persons holding a bachelor's degree earned between $17,000 and $26,000 a year in 1986 as quality assurance chemists or as assistant production managers. Food scientist-technologists may start out as junior food chemists in the research and development lab. Once they gain experience, it is possible to move into management positions.

Persons qualified at the doctorate level earned between $27,000 and $33,000 in 1986 working primarily as researchers or teachers at universities.

Job Outlook

According to Bob Weinstein, a career specialist and the author of *140 High Tech Careers* and *How to Switch Careers*:

> Opportunities for food scientist-technologists are expected to increase as expenditures for research and development within the food industry increase. As the development of new products and methods of production and distribution continue, new jobs are created. So far, growth within the food industry has been moderate, but once the federal government allocates more funds for research and development, more opportunities will be created.

CHAPTER 9

OPERATING YOUR OWN RESTAURANT

It is a possibility for you to own and operate your own restaurant. You can be the boss, make the decisions, and take responsibility for failure or success. But before considering the idea, you must realize that owning a restaurant is extremely hard work. The venture will consume all of your time—including evenings, weekends, and holidays—and at least in the beginning, it will be very expensive.

If you have seriously considered these facts, believe the reality of them, realize there is absolutely no guarantee of success, and still want to own and operate your own restaurant, congratulations. You may have made a very rewarding and lucrative decision. Here are some things you should do to avoid common downfalls and help ensure success.

GAIN RESTAURANT EXPERIENCE ELSEWHERE

If you have never worked in someone else's restaurant, you should not start one of your own.

A special personality is needed to run a restaurant. Previous work in someone else's restaurant is an excellent—and inexpensive—way to gain restaurant expertise, learn from others' mistakes, and find out if you possess the basic ingredient for successful ownership: the right kind of personality.

DEVELOP A PLAN

A restaurant owner must find property that complements the restaurant's layout and operation. Therefore, it is necessary to consider the following basic questions before choosing a specific site:

- What kind of food will be served?
- What is the general price range of food items?
- What type of service (fast food, self-service, cafeteria, counter, table service) will be offered?
- What specific menu items will be served?
- What kind of atmosphere is desired?
- Who are the anticipated clientele?
- What cooking methods will be used?
- What size staff is necessary?
- What kind of inventory is required?
- What hours will the restaurant operate?
- What are the projected sales?
- What amount of food should be prepared on site?

A Market Study

Adequate market research can help the prospective owner determine whether his or her ideas match the needs of the locale. A good market study will reveal who the potential customers are, what percentage of the population they represent, and the competition that exists. It will also help determine the business traffic patterns by hours of the day, days of the week, and a weekday versus a weekend. This knowledge will help the prospective owner supply the needs of customers and compete with existing restaurants. It will also be a big help when seeking funding from a financial institution.

The U.S. Census of Population provides demographic profiles, income levels, and housing patterns by geographic segments, right down to city blocks. The local chamber of commerce and the National Restaurant Association information service and library in Washington, D.C., have additional market research data.

Selecting a Specific Site

Location is perhaps the most deciding factor for a restaurant's success. Leave no stone unturned in scrutinizing the proper site. Ask yourself the following questions:

- Can the site be seen from the street?
- Are parking arrangements available?
- What type of businesses are nearby?
- Do taxi cabs and/or buses come by the area?
- What are the peak hours of traffic?
- Are there plans for growth in the area?
- How many households are in the area?

Sources of helpful information include the Department of Commerce, the Small Business Association, real estate agencies, restaurant consultants, accountants, bankers, and insurance agents.

Researching Codes, Ordinances, and Permits

Learn everything possible about the laws covering restaurant businesses in the area. This will preclude the possibility of being shut down or slapped with heavy fines after the restaurant opens. Some common codes include fire, health, parking, occupancy, garbage, sewage, and loading zone.

In addition, a number of licenses are necessary before opening a restaurant. Some states require a business license or a sales tax license. A fictitious name license or DBA (doing business as . . .) may be needed if the restaurant is operated under a name different from the owner's. If alcoholic beverages are on the menu, a liquor and beer and wine license is needed.

ORGANIZING YOUR RESTAURANT

Planning the Menu

Planning the menu means deciding what items to offer and what price to ask. Restaurants that can offer a limited menu and still do a high volume of business will be the most profitable. However, a limited menu sometimes restricts the restaurant's appeal and image.

Many new operations have failed because of overpricing. A general rule often used in the restaurant industry is that a menu price should not be more than double or triple the wholesale food cost.

A well-thought-out menu can serve as a guide for ordering, purchasing, and estimating income. A menu will also help determine the layout of the kitchen, the level of skill the staff needs, the level of service necessary, the amount of storage space needed, and what special equipment must be purchased.

Planning the Kitchen

The kitchen is a very important part of any restaurant, and careful planning of the kitchen can help ensure smooth operation. A good kitchen plan includes the following:

- ample work space for food preparation
- adequate space to pass food from the cooks to the food servers
- sufficient aisle space for food servers to deliver the food to the patrons
- a cleanup center for washing dishes and disposing garbage
- a separate area for inventory delivery
- an area for storage of foodstuff and linen
- proper ventilation and lighting
- reliable equipment that is easy to maintain, clean, and repair

ESTABLISHING A SOLID BUSINESS

Secure Adequate Financing

One of the major causes of restaurant failure is insufficient financing. Don't underestimate common start-up costs. These costs include wiring, plumbing, painting, labor, materials, kitchen fixtures and equipment, furniture, an initial lease deposit or down payment on property, remodeling or improvements, license payments, utility and insurance deposits, initial food inventory, initial advertising, consultant fees, such as lawyer, accountant, publicist, kitchen designer, and menu designer.

Consider Franchise Opportunities

A restaurant franchised by reputable chains has an 80-percent survival rate, compared to the 20-percent survival rate of other restaurants. Therefore, many first-time restauranteurs prefer to go this route. In recent years, it has become increasingly difficult to break into the franchise business, but it can be done.

Franchising is a form of licensing by which the owner or the franchisor obtains distribution through affiliated dealers called the franchisees.

Franchise agreements call for the parent company to give an independent businessperson rights to a successful restaurant concept and trademark as well as assistance in organizing, training, merchandising, and management. The franchisee pays the company a franchise fee and monthly royalties for these rights and assistance.

Franchisors look for people who are eager to become independent operators but who will conform to guidelines from company headquarters.

Before becoming a franchisee, one should carefully investigate the backgrounds and current business practices of the franchisor.

A reputable franchise company should provide the following:

- a site—usually a freestanding building that is leased to the franchisee
- exclusive territorial rights
- any exclusively developed equipment
- licensed use of trademark, inventory system, exclusive recipes, and techniques
- training courses and operations manuals
- continuing operations assistance for a specified percentage of gross sales
- inspections by company supervisors who will evaluate the operation
- equipment, suppliers, and advertising

Hire a Lawyer

A lawyer is a safeguard to ensure that the franchisee's interests are protected. Remember, the cost of legal advice at the outset will always be less than the cost of later representation to solve problems that could have been avoided in the beginning.

Part of the lawyer's job includes ascertaining the length of contract, royalty charges, fixed charges, purchasing requirements, quotas, arbitration privileges, contract termination, and how the company can terminate the franchisee.

BUILD A GOOD STAFF

No one succeeds alone. In the restaurant industry, this is usually the case. Operating a restaurant is not a one-person show. A good staff is critical to success.

Interviewing, hiring, and training the proper people can be a time-consuming and nerve-wracking process, but time well invested in the beginning will pay off substantially in the end.

CHAPTER 10

EDUCATIONAL REQUIREMENTS AND RESOURCES

The more training and education an individual has, the better the opportunity to begin employment at a higher level of income and responsibility. This well-known fact applies to every industry, including the restaurant business. However, the restaurant industry subscribes to the adage that experience is a great teacher. Therefore, no one has to drop out of the running because of lack of education or specific training.

More than in many other industries, restaurants offer entry-level career opportunities in great variety. The ambitious, hardworking, and career-minded individual is sure to find a route to the top in this growing industry. Thus, for the recent high school graduate who plans an immediate career start, a restaurant career is well worth considering. It is also ideal for individuals who wish to begin or change careers later in life.

Most restaurant operations are willing to invest time and money in training newcomers to the field. Once an individual has gained a sound base of knowledge, it is possible for him or her to move upward into jobs with more responsibility and better pay.

OPPORTUNITIES IN HIGH SCHOOL

Students who are still in high school can accelerate their restaurant career development by taking food service courses offered in high schools or vocational schools. These courses, depending on the type and number taken, can give the graduate an advantage when seeking employment. Also, part-time work in a restaurant while still in high school can be a valuable aid.

JUNIOR AND COMMUNITY COLLEGES

One of the richest sources of new management talent in the restaurant industry is found in junior and community colleges that offer associate degrees in various aspects of food service. Hundreds of jobs are open to graduates with this training.

Two-year college programs in food service pave the way for graduates to undertake beginning administrative and supervisory jobs in nearly any type of restaurant operation.

There are a wide variety of courses available at junior and community colleges. They include:

- food purchasing and storage
- food preparation
- menu planning
- equipment purchasing and layout
- personnel management and job analysis
- food standards and sanitations
- diet therapy
- catering
- beverage control
- food cost accounting
- record keeping

In addition to these courses, a number of general courses, designed to broaden the student's knowledge and outlook on the restaurant industry, may include the following:

- communication skills
- psychology
- sociology
- economics
- chemistry
- nutrition
- physical education

The advantage of many community and junior college programs is that they are less expensive than other college programs and they combine classroom work with practical job experience in part-time restaurant jobs.

Many restaurant owners support local college programs by providing part-time employment for students and also career opportunities for graduates.

FOUR-YEAR UNIVERSITIES OR COLLEGES

The restaurant industry's need for graduates of four-year college programs in management has never been filled. A large number of management and management training positions are open in all segments of the industry, including the following:

- assistant manager
- food production supervisor
- purchasing agent
- food cost accountant

- food service director
- director of recipe development
- sales manager
- banquet manager
- catering manager

Undergraduate programs include:

- basic and advanced courses in food preparation
- specialized courses in restaurant accounting, catering, management, and sanitation
- general courses in economics, law, marketing, cost control, and finance.

Many four-year colleges require summer work in restaurants as well. Graduates of four-year programs can receive a bachelor's degree in restaurant management.

TRAINING IN THE RESTAURANT INDUSTRY

The restaurant industry is a very competitive business. Therefore, restaurant employers offer extensive training to their workers to ensure high levels of customer satisfaction. These training programs improve restaurant business and at the same time help unskilled workers develop career potential.

Workers are trained not only for the jobs they are hired for but also for the positions they would like to advance to. Through such programs as apprenticeships, internships, mentoring, and management development initiatives, employees have the opportunity to explore their interest in and suitability for careers in the restaurant industry.

Programs of this nature offer workers with great potential but limited skills a supportive environment where they can develop the expertise needed to enhance their career options.

McDonald's Hamburger U

McDonald's Corporation, the largest restaurant organization in the world, with more than ten thousand restaurants doing business around the globe, has a worldwide management training center in Oakbrook, Illinois. It is called Hamburger University, and its main purpose is to instruct McDonald's personnel in the various aspects of its business.

Systematic training stressing "quality, service and cleanliness" to its customers is made available to all employees—from the newest crew member to the veteran restaurant manager and beyond.

The advanced operations course, targeted to employees about to become store managers, has the largest attendance. The two-week curriculum covers four major areas: equipment, store controls, human relations skills, and management skills. In addition to the advanced operations course, Hamburger U offers nine other courses for virtually every level of McDonald's management.

The university has seven major classrooms, eight seminar rooms, a library, and four full functioning equipment laboratories, all located on an eighty-acre, tree-covered site with two large man-made lakes.

The thirty resident professors, all former restaurant managers, use widely varied techniques depending on the subject matter. But basically, a classroom environment is maintained utilizing student interaction via role plays, discussion groups, and hands-on operation for the equipment courses.

Approximately three thousand students each year take Hamburger University's advanced operations course, each with the goal of advancing his or her career.

Many of McDonald's programs and courses are recommended for college credits by the American Council on Education (ACE). ACE's credit recommendations may be used to satisfy basic prerequisites at the undergraduate level of many colleges and universities.

The McDonald's Corporation sums up its management training philosophy in this way:

> From our employees, we demand enthusiasm, hard work, stick-to-the-basics, and complete dedication to the objectives of the organization. Our company provides training opportunities at all levels from trainee to executive. All of it begins with the knowledge and skills from the operating restaurant level. There is no progress for those who fail to measure up, and there is no ceiling for those who master the successive tasks.

And Burger King, Too

Burger King Corporation also has a training school to help managers advance their careers. Formerly known as Whopper College, it is now called Burger King University (BKU) and is located in Miami, Florida, at the corporation's headquarters.

Assistant managers receive training in restaurants and regional training centers throughout the country. As part of final training, before becoming a functional regional manager, employees attend BKU in Miami for one or two weeks to gain administrative and financial training. Total training lasts ten to twelve weeks.

Training covers the operational, technical, marketing, financial, and administrative aspects of the industry.

Some of the things students are taught include:

* basic bookkeeping and accounting procedures
* sanitation standards
* how to properly maintain grounds
* how to promote programs
* how to identify problems with machinery
* how to identify viable work applicants
* how to schedule personnel
* how to order inventory
* how many cash registers to have open
* how to delegate responsibility
* how to anticipate patronage
* how to prepare food products to ensure consistency from location to location

Burger King has 4,291 franchised outlets and 816 company-owned restaurants.

Pizza Hut's Minority Mentor Program

Pizza Hut, Inc., headquartered in Wichita, Kansas, began its third year-long program for newly hired minority and women managers in January 1989.

In this program, new managers are placed with personnel two levels above their rank who serve as role models. Informal contact is made every two weeks during the year to provide indoctrination into the corporate environment and to discuss problems. The mentors guide, counsel, protect, and sometimes promote the development of the junior members. Role models may be in a different department from the new manager in order to provide broader exposure to the corporation.

Pizza Hut was established in 1958. There are 2,812 franchised restaurants and 2,655 company-owned outlets.

Davidson College

In response to a need expressed by the National Association of College and University Foodservices (NACUFS), a training program was developed in 1983 by Davidson College in Davidson, North Carolina. It was aimed at college food service personnel who had little, if any, basic restaurant skills training.

According to Davidson College, in recent years many college food service personnel had come from working in fast food restaurants where the training was not as extensive as that needed to work in a college food service department.

Participants in the program were recruited from member schools of NACUFS. Instruction was provided by working chefs from the schools.

When the program started, two-day workshops were given during Thanksgiving and Christmas holidays. The program was later extended to three days and held during the summer. Hands-on instruction is given in six basic culinary skills: knife handling, garnishing, sauce preparation, identification of cuts of meat, cake decoration, and meat carving.

Students who complete the training receive a certificate of completion and a French knife to symbolize their newly acquired cooking expertise.

For more information contact the Foodservice Director, Davidson College, Davidson, North Carolina 28036, (704) 892-2000.

CHAPTER 11

EMPLOYEE BENEFITS

Currently, the restaurant industry is experiencing a decrease in the available labor pool. This means there are more jobs available in the restaurant industry than there are people to perform those jobs. Because an eating establishment cannot operate without qualified workers, restaurant employers are offering higher salaries and more attractive benefit packages.

In many areas of the country, restaurant workers are reaping the rewards of employees who realize that the minimum wage is no longer a viable compensation to attract hard-working, entry-level employees. In addition to competitive wages to hire and retain the most qualified workers, employers are now using benefit and incentive programs. In fact, many restaurants are accepting benefit and incentive programs as a required cost of doing business.

These incentive programs benefit both restaurant workers and employers. According to MDR Associates in Fairfax, Virginia, a professional hospitality management consulting firm, a properly organized and implemented benefit and incentive program can work as a marketing tool to help employers accomplish the following objectives:

- attract and retain the most talented people for the organization
- improve overall employee relations
- increase employee morale, motivation, and performance
- reduce employee absenteeism from the job
- reduce overtime hours necessary because of absenteeism
- decrease employee turnover
- generate cost savings because less time is spent on training new staff

Benefit and incentive programs offered to restaurant employees can vary from operation to operation. Some of the more common benefits offered include the following:

Medical and health-related programs. Included in such programs are hospital, surgical, accident, and major medical and dental insurance plans. Sometimes, additional health programs are administered by the employer to include contributory payments for those items not covered by the standard plans, such as physical examinations, clinic visits, routine dental services, vision and auditory exams, and blood bank usage costs.

Insurance programs. Group life, individual life, accidental death/dismemberment, long- and short-term disability and travel-accident policies are commonly awarded benefits for older, management-level employees.

Additional pay programs. Overtime, extra shifts, and/or holiday, sick, and vacation pay come under this heading.

Educational assistance. Operators who require large numbers of young workers have found educational assistance to be a very effective employee lure. An educational assistance program might include tuition aid contributions or scholarship awards for those employees attending or planning to attend college.

Education programs that are aimed at increasing an employee's knowledge of his or her current job or of the overall industry benefit both the employer and the employee. On-the-job training programs, attendance at local industry seminars, and paid subscriptions to industry journals are also common examples of benefits in this area.

Employee counseling. Some restaurants participate in referral counseling programs such as alcohol/drug assistance, personal/emotional counseling, financial/credit management assistance, legal services, and preretirement counseling.

Child care. Because private child care facilities are too expensive for all but the largest corporate organizations, small or independent restaurant operators who recognize the increasing role that working mothers play in the restaurant industry work force have implemented the following programs to assist the parents on their staffs:

- a referral program of nearby licensed child-care centers
- contributions to child-care costs
- flexible hours and/or responsibilities for those workers who must provide transportation to and from day-care centers
- sick-child days given as personal, unpaid leave time without affecting seniority or accrual of benefits
- maternity and paternity leave after the birth of a child, again without compromising seniority.

Performance incentives. The most cost-effective benefit and incentive program is a system of awards and bonuses given for desired performance. These performance incentives can take the form of length-of-service awards, idea/suggestion box awards, productivity awards, and safety commendations.

Profit sharing. Probably one of the greatest performance incentives is profit sharing. According to a 1985 compensation and benefit study by Laventhol and Horwath for the National Restaurant Association, 17 percent of restaurants have some form of profit-sharing plan. (There is good reason to believe that the percentage has increased.) Companies using a profit-sharing plan have reported that it has resulted in measurable benefits, such as a decrease in absenteeism, tardiness, and turnover, and an increase in productivity, employee interest, and effort. Profit sharing also encourages acceptance of change and new technology and, in fact, any action that might increase profits. It also promotes teamwork among employees, management, and stockholders by providing a single objective for unified attention.

In addition, a number of restaurants offer the following benefits and incentives:

- bereavement leave and pay
- Christmas party
- coffee breaks
- credit union memberships
- direct deposit of payroll checks
- discounts to employee family members
- flexible hours
- health club corporate membership
- holiday turkey or ham
- jury duty leave
- locker room/shower facilities
- meal allowances
- parking cost assistance
- recreational activities

- relocation expense reimbursement
- safety commendations
- summer picnic
- trade journals and periodicals
- transportation cost assistance
- uniform/dry cleaning allowance
- vending machines
- well-pay programs

In the future, more comprehensive food service training will be offered in hotel, restaurant, and institutional programs. (School of Hotel Administration photo)

CHAPTER 12

THE FUTURE OF THE RESTAURANT INDUSTRY

What will the restaurant industry be like in the next century? To help restaurant operators answer this question, the National Restaurant Association embarked, in early 1988, on a futuristic study of the restaurant industry in the year 2000.

By employing the Delphi approach—a research method that uses a panel of industry experts to identify and analyze issues by subjective judgments rather than precise analytical techniques— the NRA study provides a unique glimpse of the restaurant industry at the turn of the century. This survey is intended to aid restaurant operators in planning efforts. It will also provide helpful insights to those individuals who are considering a career in the restaurant industry.

Here are some of the findings of NRA's *Current Issues Report: Foodservice Industry 2000.*

INDUSTRY STRUCTURE IN THE YEAR 2000

Competition will intensify; more than 85 percent of the panel participants said that competition in the restaurant industry will be more intense than it is today, with new forms of competition arising from grocery stores and convenience stores. Unit expansion is forecast to show slower growth than in the 1980s. Overall industry sales growth is expected to continue but could be slower than in the 1980s.

Chain growth will continue; panelists predicted that the chains will increase their share of both sales and units. This will come mainly through mergers and acquisitions rather than internal growth.

Delphi members indicated that fast food operations will continue to play an important role in the industry, with this segment garnering an increased share of food service sales. Also, food service contractors are likely to capture a greater share of the institutional market, a segment that is predicted to expand more rapidly than at present.

Panelists noted the possibility that more regional restaurant chains could emerge, due to the flexibility of smaller, local chain operators to adapt to local consumer dining preferences.

Entrepreneurs remain important; 80 percent of the panel indicated that the independent restaurant entrepreneur would be the primary source of new dining concepts at the turn of the century. Panelists also noted that concepts such as food boutiques and gourmet-to-go meals will be more prominent, which seems logical in light of the panelists' forecast that off-premise consumption by consumers will grow to capture a larger share of the total food service industry sales.

THE WORK FORCE IN THE YEAR 2000

More Training and Development

More than 93 percent of the panelists said that the industry will provide more training programs for its workers—both within the food service organizations and within hotel, restaurant, and institutional educational programs.

Training Methods

In addition to forecasting that future restaurant industry management will be more highly educated, panelists said that a greater emphasis will be placed on developing career options for the industry's workers. These training methods are expected to be more sophisticated and comprehensive and rely more on the use of video and compact discs as an instructional medium.

Participants also said that corporations could be expected to increase their financial support of educational institutions that provide restaurant training.

The Role of Educational Institutions

Almost 89 percent of the panelists believed that more comprehensive food service training will be offered in hotel, restaurant, and institutional (HRI) programs. More cooks and chefs are expected to have more culinary training. More restaurant employees could elect for a career as opposed to a mere job in the industry due to more and better HRI programs. However, this increased emphasis on the training, development, and education of the typical restaurant employee does not mean that the industry's current turnover problems will be alleviated.

Turnover

Over half of the Delphi panelists expect the industry problem with employee turnover to remain an issue in the year 2000. However, the panelists do predict that tomorrow's workers will be older, and the industry will employ a larger proportion of women and minority groups.

Productivity Emphasis

Because of a tight labor market, Delphi panelists agree that more emphasis will be placed on increasing employee productivity. The industry will turn to technological improvements and advances to aid industry productivity in the year 2000. In addition, restaurant operators could provide employees with greater flexibility in the hours worked and increase their use of part-time workers in the work force.

Some panelists said they believed that fewer employees might be needed at restaurants because an increasing number of customers will be using take-out and delivery services instead of eating at the restaurant.

SCHOOLS OFFERING PROGRAMS IN HOTEL, RESTAURANT, AND INSTITUTIONAL MANAGEMENT

In the past, many restaurant employees learned their occupation by starting at the bottom job at the establishment and working their way up. For many, this process took a long time. Now there are academic programs designed to provide the training essential for nearly any job an aspiring worker seeks.

Even for the worker who fills entry-level jobs that require no prior experience, promotion to higher-level jobs is gained faster when education is added to experience. Individuals trying to advance into top and mid-management positions can enhance their prospects by preparing themselves educationally. In many instances, education may be substituted for experience on a year-for-year basis.

Large restaurants and restaurant chains are currently placing more emphasis on education and formal training as the fast pace and competition in the business community continue. Recruiters from these restaurants go to colleges to interview students graduating with degrees in the field.

The information in this appendix is taken from an extensive survey conducted by the National Restaurant Association and the National Institute for the Foodservice Industry.

Additional information for most of the schools listed is available from NRA and NIFI including:

- number of students enrolled
- number of faculty members
- names of program directors
- costs
- brief program descriptions

The title of the program is included with each school's listing. Although programs vary greatly, there appear to be two general categories of programs: one in the area of hospitality (hotel and restaurant management) and the other in the area of culinary arts and commercial cooking. Many schools offer both categories.

It is suggested that each school be contacted directly for more detailed and the most current information on its program.

Alabama

Community College of the
   Air Force
Restaurant Management
CCAF/AYL Building 836
Maxwell AFB, Alabama
   36112
(205) 293-6447

Bessemer State Technical
   College
Food Service
P.O. Box 308
Bessemer, Alabama 35021
(205) 428-6391

Carver State Technical College
   Food Preparation and
      Services
   414 Stanton Street
   Mobile, Alabama 36617
   (205) 473-8692

Jefferson State Junior College
   Food Service Management
      and Technology
   2601 Carson Road
   Birmingham, Alabama
      35215
   (205) 853-1200

Lawson State Community
College
Commercial Food
Preparation
3060 Wilson Road, S.W.
Birmingham, Alabama
35221
(205) 925-1666

Wallace State Community
College
Quality Foods and Nutrition
P.O. Box 250
Hanceville, Alabama 35077
(205) 352-6403

Alaska

Anchorage Community
College
Food Service Technology
2533 Providence Avenue
Anchorage, Alaska 99504
(907) 263-1402

Arizona

Pima Community College
Hospitality Education
Program
P.O. Box 5027
Tucson, Arizona 85703
(602) 884-6541

Phoenix College
Foodservice Administration
1202 W. Thomas Road
Phoenix, Arizona 85013
(602) 264-2492

Scottsdale Community
College
Hospitality Program
9000 E. Chaparral Road
Scottsdale, Arizona 85253
(602) 941-0999

Arkansas

Quapaw Vocational Technical
Food Service Management
201 Vo-Tech Drive
Hot Springs, Arkansas
71913
(501) 767-9314

Southern Arkansas
University–Technical
Branch
Hotel and Restaurant
Management
P.O. Box 3048
Camden, Arkansas 71701
(501) 574-0741

California

American River College
  Food Service Management
  4700 College Oak Drive
  Sacramento, California
    95841
  (916) 484-8145

Bakersfield College
  Hotel, Restaurant and
    Institutional Management
  1801 Panorama Drive
  Bakersfield, California
    93305
  (805) 395-4561

California Culinary Academy
  Professional Chef Program
  215 Fremont Street
  San Francisco, California
    94105
  (415) 543-2764

Canada College
  Hotel, Restaurant and
    Institutional Management
  4200 Farm Hill Boulevard
  Redwood City, California
    94061
  (415) 364-1212

Chaffey Community College
  Food Service Management
    Training
  5885 Haven
  Alta Loma, California
    91701
  (714) 987-1737

Columbia College
  Hospitality Management
  P.O. Box 1849
  Columbia, California 95310
  (209) 532-3141

Contra Costa College
  Culinary Arts
  2600 Mission Bell Drive
  San Pablo, California 94806
  (415) 235-7800

Cypress College
  Culinary Arts Department
  9200 Valley View
    Boulevard
  Cypress, California 90630
  (714) 826-2220

College of the Desert
  School of Culinary Arts
  43500 Monterey Avenue
  Palm Desert, California
    92260
  (619) 346-8041

Diablo Valley College
Hotel and Restaurant
   Management Program
321 Golf Club Road
Pleasant Hill, California
   94523
(415) 685-1230

El Camino College
Food Service Management
16007 Crenshaw Boulevard
Torrance, California 90506
(213) 532-3670

Glendale Community College
Food Service and
   Management Program
1500 North Verdugo Road
Glendale, California 91208
(213) 240-1000

Grossmont College
Food Service Management
8800 Grossmont College
   Drive
El Cajon, California 92020
(714) 465-1700

Lake Tahoe Community
   College
Innkeeping and Restaurant
   Operations
P.O. Box 14445
South Lake Tahoe,
   California 95602
(916) 541-4660

Laney Community College
Food Preparation and
   Service
900 Fallon Street
Oakland, California 94607
(415) 834-5740

Los Angeles City College
Family and Consumer
   Studies
855 N. Vermont Avenue
Los Angeles, California
   90029
(213) 669-4235

Los Angeles Trade–Technical
   College
Hotel–Motel
   Management/Culinary
   Arts
400 W. Washington
   Boulevard
Los Angeles, California
   90015
(213) 746-0800

Merced College
Home Economics
3600 M Street
Merced, California 95340
(209) 723-4321

Modesto Junior College
Food Service
West Campus–Blue Gum
Avenue
Modesto, California 95350
(209) 526-2000

Orange Coast College
Food Service and Hotel
Management
2701 Fairview Road
Costa Mesa, California
92626
(714) 556-5876

Oxnard College
Hotel and Restaurant
Management
4000 S. Rose Avenue
Oxnard, California 93033
(805) 488-0911

Pasadena City College
Food Service Instruction
1570 E. Colorado
Boulevard
Pasadena, California 91106
(213) 578-7235

Saddleback College
Hospitality Management
5500 Irvine Center Drive
Irvine, California 72714
(714) 559-9300

San Diego Community
College District
Food Services/Hotel, Motel
Management
3375 Camino Del Rio South
San Diego, California
92108
(619) 230-2084

San Diego Mesa College
Hotel, Motel Management
7250 Mesa College Drive
San Diego, California
92111
(714) 279-2300

City College of San Francisco
Hotel and Restaurant
Department
50 Phelan Avenue
San Francisco, California
94112
(415) 239-3152

San Joaquin Delta
Community College
Food Service Industry
5151 Pacific Avenue
Stockton, California 95207
(209) 472-5519

Santa Barbara City College
Hotel and Restaurant
Management
721 Cliff Drive
Santa Barbara, California
93109
(805) 965-0581

Shasta College
Foodservice and Culinary
Arts
1065 N. Old Oregon Trail
Redding, California 96099
(916) 221-0742

Ventura College
Food Management
4667 Telegraph Road
Ventura, California 93003
(805) 642-3211

West Valley College
Food Service Restaurant
Management
14000 Fruitvale Avenue
Saratoga, California 95070
(408) 867-2200

Yuba Community College
Food Service Management
2088 N. Beale Road
Marysville, California
95901
(916) 742-7351

Colorado

Community College of the
Air Force
Restaurant
Management/Management–
Logistics Department
3440th Technical Training
Group
Lowry AFB, Colorado
80230
(303) 370-3211

Aurora Public School
Technical Center
Food Management Training
500 Buckley Road
Aurora, Colorado 80011
(303) 344-4910

Colorado Mountain
College/Timberline
Campus
Ski/Resort Management
Leadville, Colorado 80461
(303) 486-2015

Front Range Community
College
Dietetic Technology
3645 W. 112th Avenue
Westminster, Colorado
80030
(303) 466-8811

Emily Griffith Opportunity
School
Denver Public School
System
Foodservice Production and
Management
1250 Welton Street
Denver, Colorado 80204
(303) 572-8218

Pikes Peak Community
College
Food Management Program
5675 S. Academy
Boulevard
Colorado Springs,
Colorado 80906
(303) 576-7711

Connecticut

Manchester Community
College
Hotel and Food Service
Management Program
60 Bidwell Street
Manchester, Connecticut
06040
(203) 646-4900

Mattatuck Community
College
Culinary Arts
750 Chase Parkway
Waterbury, Connecticut
06708
(203) 575-8036

University of New Haven
Hotel/Restaurant
Management
300 Orange Avenue
West Haven, Connecticut
06516
(203) 934-6321

South Central Community
College
Dietetic
Technician/Nutrition Care
60 Sargent Drive
New Haven, Connecticut
06511
(203) 789-7826

Delaware

Delaware Technical
Community College
Hospitality Management
P.O. Box 610
Georgetown, Delaware
19947
(302) 856-5400

Widener University
  Hotel and Restaurant
  Management
  P.O. Box 7139–Concord
  Pike
  Wilmington, Delaware
  19803
  (302) 478-3000

Florida

Atlantic Vocational Technical
  Center
  Culinary Arts
  4700 N.W. Coconut Creek
  Parkway
  Coconut Creek, Florida
  33066
  (305) 979-6220

Broward Community College
  Restaurant Management;
  Hotel–Motel
  Administration
  3502 S.W. Davie Road
  Fort Lauderdale, Florida
  33314
  (305) 475-6710

Daytona Beach Community
  College
  Hospitality Management
  P.O. Box 1111
  Daytona Beach, Florida
  32015
  (904) 255-8131

Florida Junior College at
  Jacksonville
  Hospitality Management
  3939 Roosevelt Boulevard
  Jacksonville, Florida 32205
  (904) 387-8166

Gulf Coast Community
  College
  Hotel–Motel, Restaurant
  Management
  5230 W. Highway 98
  Panama City, Florida 32401
  (904) 769-1551

Hillsborough Community
  College
  Hotel and Restaurant
  Management
  P.O. Box 22127
  Tampa, Florida 33622
  (813) 879-7222

Manatee Junior College
Food Service–Restaurant
Hotel–Motel Management
5840 26th Street, West
Bradenton, Florida 33507
(813) 755-1511

Miami–Dade Community
College
Hotel, Restaurant and
Institutional Management
300 N.E. Second Avenue
Miami, Florida 33132
(305) 577-6800

Mid-Florida Technical
Institute
Hospitality Program
2900 W. Oakridge Road
Orlando, Florida 32809
(305) 855-5880

North Technical Education
Center
Culinary Arts
7071 Garden Road
Riviera Beach, Florida
33404
(305) 848-0692

Okaloosa–Walton Junior
College
Commercial
Foods–Industrial
Education
100 College Boulevard
Niceville, Florida 32578
(904) 678-5111

Palm Beach Junior College
Hospitality Management
Program
4200 S. Congress Avenue
Lake Worth, Florida 33461
(305) 439-8162

College of the Palm Beaches
Hotel–Motel Management
660 Fern Street
W. Palm Beach, Florida
33401
(305) 833-5575

Pensacola Junior College
Dietetic Technician/Hotel
and Restaurant
Management
1000 College Boulevard
Pensacola, Florida 32504
(904) 476-5410

Pinellas Vocational Technical
    Institute
Culinary Arts Department
6100 154th Avenue, North
Clearwater, Florida 33540
(813) 535-3531

Sarasota County Vocational
    Technical Center
Culinary Arts/Hospitality
    Management
4748 Beneva Road
Sarasota, Florida 33583
(813) 924-1365

Seminole Community College
Food Service/Culinary Arts
Highway 17-92
Sanford, Florida 32771
(305) 323-1450

St. Augustine Technical
    Center
Commercial
    Foods/Culinary Arts
    Program
Collins Avenue at Del
    Monte Drive
St. Augustine, Florida
    32084
(904) 824-4401

St. Petersburg Junior College
Hospitality Management
P.O. Box 13489
St. Petersburg, Florida
    33733
(813) 381-0681

Valencia Community College
Hotel, Motel and
    Restaurant Management
    Training
P.O. Box 3028
Orlando, Florida 32802
(305) 299-5000

Webber College
Hospitality Management
Route 27-A
Babson Park, Florida 33827
(813) 638-1431

Georgia

Ben Hill–Irwin Area
    Vocational Technical
    School
Food Service
P.O. Box 1069
Fitzgerald, Georgia 31750
(912) 468-7487

Georgia State University
  Hotel, Restaurant and
    Travel Administration
  University Plaza
  Atlanta, Georgia 30303
  (404) 658-3512

Houston Vocational Center
  Food Service Department
  1311 Corder Road
  Warner Robins, Georgia
    31056
  (912) 922-4231

Macon Area Vocational
    Technical School
  Quantity Food Service
  3300 Macon Tech Drive
  Macon, Georgia 31206
  (912) 781-0551

Hawaii

Cannon's International
    Business College of
    Honolulu
  Hotel Front Office
    Procedures, Hotel
    Management
  33 S. King Street
  Honolulu, Hawaii 96813
  (808) 521-5333

Hawaii Community College
  Food Service Department
  1175 Manono Street
  Hilo, Hawaii 96720
  (808) 961-9432

Honolulu Community College
  Commercial Baking
  874 Dillingham Boulevard
  Honolulu, Hawaii 96817
  (808) 845-9138

Kapiolani Community College
  Food Service and
    Hospitality Education
  620 Pensacola Street
  Honolulu, Hawaii 96814
  (808) 531-4654

Leeward Community College
  Food Service Program,
    Vocational Technical
    Division
  96-045 Ala Ike
  Pearl City, Hawaii 96782
  (808) 455-0011

Maui Community College
  Food Service Program
  310 Kaahumanu Avenue
  Kahului, Hawaii 96732
  (808) 244-9181

Brigham Young
University—Hawaii
Travel, Hotel and
Restaurant Management
55-220 Julanui Street
Laie, Hawaii 96762
(808) 293-3211

Idaho

Boise State University
Food Service Technology
1910 University Drive
Boise, Idaho 83725
(208) 385-1957

Illinois

Chicago Hospitality Institute
Chicago City-Wide College
Foodservice and
Hotel–Motel Management
30 E. Lake Street
Chicago, Illinois 60601
(312) 781-9430

College of DuPage
Foodservice
Administration/Hotel–
Motel Management
22d Street and Lambert
Road
Glyn Ellyn, Illinois 60137
(312) 858-2800

Elgin Community College
Hospitality Management
1700 Spartan Drive
Elgin, Illinois 60120
(312) 697-1000

William Rainey Harper
College
Food Service Management,
Cooking and Baking
Algonquin and Roselle
Roads
Palatine, Illinois 60067
(312) 397-3000

Joliet Junior College
Culinary
Arts/Hotel–Restaurant
Management
1216 Houbolt Avenue
Joliet, Illinois 60436
(815) 729-9020

Kennedy–King College
Food Management
6800 S. Wentworth Avenue
Chicago, Illinois 60621
(312) 962-3200

Lexington Institute
Food Service and Lodging
Program
10840 S. Western Avenue
Chicago, Illinois 60643
(312) 779-3800

Lincoln Trail College
Restaurant
Management/Culinary
Arts
R.R. 3
Robinson, Illinois 62454
(618) 544-8657

Oakton Community College
Hotel–Motel Management
Program
1600 E. Golf Road
Des Plaines, Illinois 60016
(312) 635-1869

Parkland College
Food Service Management
2400 W. Bradley
Champaign, Illinois 61821
(217) 351-2200

Sauk Valley College
Public Services–Food
Services
R.R. 5
Dixon, Illinois 61021
(815) 288-5511

Southeastern Illinois College
Food Service Technology
R.R. 4
Harrisburg, Illinois 62946
(618) 252-4281

Triton College
Hospitality Industry
Administration
2000 Fifth Avenue
River Grove, Illinois 60171
(312) 456-0300

Washburne Trade School
Chef Training
3233 W. 31st Street
Chicago, Illinois 60623
(312) 641-4800

John Wood Community
College
Occupational Education
1919 N. 18th Street
Quincy, Illinois 62301
(217) 224-6500

Indiana

Indiana University–Purdue
  University at Indianapolis
  Restaurant, Hotel and
  Institutional Management
799 W. Michigan Street
Indianapolis, Indiana 46241
(317) 264-8772

Ivy Tech
  Hospitality Careers
1315 E. Washington Street
Indianapolis, Indiana 46202
(317) 635-6100

Purdue University
  Restaurant, Hotel and
  Institutional Management
Stone Hall
West Lafayette, Indiana
  47907
(317) 494-4643

Vincennes University
  Restaurant and Food
  Service Management
First Street
Vincennes, Indiana 47591
(812) 885-4465

Iowa

Des Moines Area Community
  College
  Hospitality Careers
2006 Ankeny Boulevard
Ankeny, Iowa 50021
(515) 964-6532

Indian Hills Community
  College
  Chef Training, Bakery
  Training
Grandview and Elm
Ottumwa, Iowa 52501
(515) 683-5197

Iowa Lakes Community
  College
  Hotel–Motel and Restaurant
  Management
3200 College Drive
Emmetsburg, Iowa 50536
(712) 852-3554

Iowa Western Community
  College
  Food Service Management;
  Cooking and Baking
2700 College Road
Council Bluffs, Iowa 51501
(712) 325-3277

Kirkwood Community College
Food Service Management
6301 Kirkwood Boulevard
S.W.
Cedar Rapids, Iowa 52406
(319) 398-5468

Kansas

Butler County Community
College
Food Service and
Management
Towanda Avenue and
Haverhill Road
El Dorado, Kansas 67042
(316) 321-5083

Central College
Food Service/Home
Economics
1200 S. Main
McPherson, Kansas 67460
(316) 241-0723

Johnson County Community
College
Hospitality Management
Program
12345 College at Quivira
Overland Park, Kansas
66210
(913) 888-8500

Manhattan Area Vocational
Technical School
Foodservice and
Management
3136 Dickens Avenue
Manhattan, Kansas 66502
(913) 539-7471

Northeast Kansas Area
Vocational Technical
School
Commercial Food
Preparation/Restaurant
Management
1501 W. Riley
Atchison, Kansas 66002
(913) 367-6204

Southwest Kansas Area
Vocational Technical
School
Foodservice Program
Second and Comanche
Streets
Dodge City, Kansas 67801
(316) 225-0285

Wichita Area Vocational
Technical School
Food Service
Mid-Management and
Culinary Arts
324 N. Emporia
Wichita, Kansas 67202
(316) 265-8666

Kentucky

Daviess County State
Vocational Technical
School
Commercial Foods
1901 S.E. Parkway
Owensboro, Kentucky
42301
(502) 684-7211

Elizabethtown State
Vocational Technical
School
Commercial Foods
505 University Drive
Elizabethtown, Kentucky
42701
(502) 765-2104

Jefferson Community College
Culinary Arts
109 E. Broadway
Louisville, Kentucky 40202
(502) 584-0181

Northern Kentucky State
Vocational Technical
School
Commercial Foods Program
Amsterdam Road
Covington, Kentucky 41011
(606) 292-2711

West Kentucky State
Vocational Technical
School
Commercial Foods
Blandville Road
P.O. Box 7408
Paducah, Kentucky 42001
(502) 554-4991

Louisiana

Baton Rouge Vocational
Technical Institute
Culinary Arts
3250 N. Acadian
Throughway
Baton Rouge, Louisiana
70805
(504) 355-5621

Sidney N. Collier Vocational
Technical Institute
Culinary Arts
3727 Louisa Street
New Orleans, Louisiana
70126
(504) 945-8080

New Orleans Regional
    Vocational Technical
    Institute
    Chef Apprenticeship
    980 Navarre Avenue
    New Orleans, Louisiana
        70124
    (504) 483-4666

Nicholls State University
    Food Service Management
    P.O. Box 2014 NSU
    Thibodaux, Louisiana
        70301
    (504) 446-8111

Maine

Eastern Maine Vocational
    Technical Institute
    Food Technology
    354 Hogan Road
    Bangor, Maine 04401
    (207) 942-5217

Southern Maine Vocational
    Technical Institute
    Culinary Arts/Hotel, Motel
    and Restaurant
    Management
    2 Fort Road
    South Portland, Maine
        04106
    (207) 799-7303

Maryland

Baltimore's International
    Culinary Arts Institute
    Restaurant Skills, Baking
    and Pastry Skills
    19 South Gay Street
    Baltimore, Maryland 21202
    (301) 752-4710

Essex Community College
    Hotel–Motel and
    Restaurant–Club
    Management
    7201 Rossville Boulevard
    Baltimore, Maryland 21237
    (301) 522-1456

Hagerstown Junior College
    Hospitality Program
    751 Robinwood Drive
    Hagerstown, Maryland
        21740
    (301) 790-2800

Montgomery College
    Hospitality Management
    51 Mannakee Street
    Rockville, Maryland 20850
    (301) 279-5185

Wor-Wic Tech Community
College
Hotel, Motel and
Restaurant Management
Route 3, Box 79
Berlin, Maryland 21811
(301) 641-4134

Massachusetts

Berkshire Community College
Hotel and Restaurant
Management
West Street
Pittsfield, Massachusetts
01201
(413) 499-4660

Bunker Hill Community
College
Hotel/Restaurant
Management/Culinary
Arts
New Rutherford Avenue
Charlestown,
Massachusetts 02129
(617) 241-8600

Cape Cod Community College
Hotel/Restaurant
Management Program
Route 132
West Barnstable,
Massachusetts 02668
(617) 362-1231

Chamberlayne Junior College
Hotel and Institutional
Management
128 Commonwealth Avenue
Boston, Massachusetts
02116
(617) 536-4500

Endicott College
Hotel–Restaurant
Management
376 Hale Street
Beverly, Massachusetts
01915
(617) 927-0585

Holyoke Community College
Hospitality Management
Program
303 Homestead Avenue
Holyoke, Massachusetts
01040
(413) 538-7000

Laboure Junior College
  Division of Dietetic
    Technology
  2120 Dorchester Avenue
  Boston, Massachusetts
    02124
  (617) 296-8300

Newbury Junior College
  Culinary Arts Program
  129 Fisher Avenue
  Brookline, Massachusetts
    02146
  (617) 739-0510

Northeastern University
  Hotel and Restaurant
    Management
  102 Churchill Hall
  Boston, Massachusetts
    02115
  (617) 437-2407

Henry O. Peabody School
  Culinary Arts
  Nichols Street and Peabody
    Road
  Norwood, Massachusetts
    02062
  (617) 762-7461

Quincy Junior College
  Hotel/Restaurant
    Management
  34 Coddington Street
  Quincy, Massachusetts
    02169
  (617) 786-8777

Michigan

The Career Development
    Center
  Culinary Arts
  5961 14th Street
  Detroit, Michigan 48217
  (313) 894-0610

Davenport College of Business
  Hospitality Management
  415 E. Fulton Street
  Grand Rapids, Michigan
    49503
  (616) 451-3511

Ferris State College
  Food Service/Hospitality
    Management
  South Commons
  Big Rapids, Michigan
    49307
  (616) 796-0461

Henry Ford Community
   College
   Culinary Arts/Hotel
      Restaurant Management
   5101 Evergreen Road
   Dearborn, Michigan 48128
   (313) 271-2750

Gogebic Community College
   Food Service
   Jackson and Greenbush
   Ironwood, Michigan 49938
   (906) 932-4231

Grand Rapids Junior College
   Hotel/Restaurant
      Management; Culinary
      Arts
   143 Bostwick N.E.
   Grand Rapids, Michigan
      49503
   (616) 456-4837

Lake Michigan College
   Food Service Management
   2755 East Napier Avenue
   Benton Harbor, Michigan
      49022
   (616) 927-3571

Lansing Community College
   Food Service and
      Hotel/Motel Management
   419 North Capitol Avenue
   Lansing, Michigan 48901
   (517) 483-1561

Macomb Community College
   Professional Foodservice
   44575 Garfield Road
   Mount Clemens, Michigan
      48044
   (313) 286-2000

Charles S. Mott Community
      College
   Food Management
   1401 E. Court Street
   Flint, Michigan 48502
   (313) 762-0440

Northwestern Michigan
      College
   Food Services Technology
   1701 E. Front Street
   Traverse City, Michigan
      49684
   (616) 946-5650

Northwood Institute–Michigan
   Hotel/Restaurant Operation
   3225 Cook Road
   Midland, Michigan 48640
   (517) 631-1660

Oakland Community College
Hospitality Department
27055 Orchard Lake Road
Farmington Hills,
Michigan 48018
(313) 471-7779

Schoolcraft Community
College
Culinary Arts
18600 Haggerty Road
Livonia, Michigan 48152
(313) 591-6400

Siena Heights College
Hotel, Restaurant and
Institutional Management
1247 E. Siena Heights
Drive
Adrian, Michigan 49221
(517) 263-0731

St. Clair County Community
College
Foodservice
Management/Vocational
323 Erie Street
Port Huron, Michigan
48060
(313) 984-3881

State Technical Institute
Food Service Training
Alber Drive
Plainwell, Michigan 49080
(616) 664-3361

Washtenaw Community
College
Foods and Hospitality
4800 E. Huron River Drive
Ann Arbor, Michigan
48106
(313) 973-3584

Wayne County Community
College
Culinary Arts Program
8551 Greenfield
Detroit, Michigan 48228
(313) 496-2655

West Shore Community
College
Hospitality Management
3000 N. Stiles Road
Scottville, Michigan 49454
(616) 845-6211

Minnesota

Alexandria Area Vocational
Technical Institute
Hotel, Motel and
Restaurant Management
1601 Jefferson Street
Alexandria, Minnesota
56308
(612) 762-0221

Canby Area Vocational
Technical Institute
Food Service Management
1011 First Street West
Canby, Minnesota 56220
(507) 223-7252

Dakota County Area
Vocational Technical
Institute
Food Service and Chef
Management
1301 145th Street East
Rosemount, Minnesota
55068
(612) 423-8301

Detroit Lakes Area Vocational
Technical Institute
Commercial Cooking and
Baking
Highway 34 East
Detroit Lakes, Minnesota
56501
(218) 847-1341

Duluth Area Vocational
Technical Institute
Food Service Management
2101 Trinity Road
Duluth, Minnesota 55811
(218) 722-2801

Hennepin Technical Centers
Cook/Chef
1820 N. Xenium Lane
Minneapolis, Minnesota
55441
(612) 559-3535

Mankato Area Vocational
Technical Institute
Cook/Chef
1920 Lee Boulevard
North Mankato, Minnesota
56001
(507) 625-3441

University of Minnesota
Technical
College–Crookston
Hotel, Restaurant and
Institutional Management
Highway 2 and 75, North
Crookston, Minnesota
56716
(218) 281-6510

Moorhead Area Vocational
Technical Institute
Chef Training
1900 28th Avenue South
Moorhead, Minnesota
56560
(218) 236-6277

Normandale Community
  College
Hospitality Management
  Program
9700 France Avenue South
Bloomington, Minnesota
  55431
(612) 830-9300

Willmar Area Vocational
  Technical Institute
Chefs Training and Food
  Service Management
Box 1097
Willmar, Minnesota 56201
(612) 235-5114

916 Vocational Technical
  Institute
Chef Training
3300 Century Avenue North
White Bear Lake,
  Minnesota 55110
(612) 770-2351

Meridian Junior College
Hotel and Restaurant
  Management
5500 Highway 19 North
Meridian, Mississippi
  39305
(601) 483-8241

Mississippi Gulf Coast Junior
  College–Jefferson Davis
  Campus
Hotel, Motel and
  Restaurant Program
Handsboro Station
Gulfport, Mississippi 39501
(601) 896-3355

The Northeast Mississippi
  Junior College
Hotel, Motel and
  Restaurant Management
Booneville, Mississippi
  38829
(601) 728-7751

Mississippi

Hinds Junior College
Hotel, Motel and
  Restaurant Management
3925 Sunset Drive
Jackson, Mississippi 39213
(601) 366-1405

Missouri

Crowder College
Hotel, Motel and
  Restaurant Program
Neosho, Missouri 64850
(471) 451-3223

Jefferson College
  Hotel/Restaurant
    Management
  Hillsboro, Missouri 63050
  (314) 789-3951

Pann Valley Community
    College
  Lodging and Food Service
    Management
  3201 Southwest Trafficway
  Kansas City, Missouri
    64111
  (816) 932-7600

St. Louis Community College
    at Florissant Valley
  Dietetic Technology
  3400 Pershall Road
  St. Louis, Missouri 63135
  (314) 595-4426

St. Louis Community College
    at Forest Park
  Hospitality Restaurant
    Management Department
  5600 Oakland Avenue
  St. Louis, Missouri 63110
  (314) 644-9749

State Fair Community College
  Food Service Management
  1900 Clarendon Road
  Sedalia, Missouri 65301
  (816) 826-7100

Three Rivers Community
    College
  Hospitality Management
    Program
  Three Rivers Boulevard
  Poplar Bluff, Missouri
    63901
  (314) 686-4101

Montana

Missoula Vocational
    Technical Center
  Food Service
  909 South Avenue West
  Missoula, Montana 59803
  (406) 721-1330

Western Montana College
  Institutions and Resort
    Management
  710 S. Atlantic
  Dillon, Montana 59725
  (406) 683-7011

Nebraska

Central Community College
  Hotel and Restaurant
    Management
  P.O. Box 1024
  Hastings, Nebraska 68901
  (402) 463-3745

Metropolitan Technical
    Community College
Culinary Arts
P.O. Box 3777
Omaha, Nebraska 68103
(402) 499-8400

Southeast Community
    College–Lincoln Campus
Food Service Management
8800 ''O'' Street
Lincoln, Nebraska 68520
(402) 471-3333

Nevada

Truckee Meadows
    Community College
Food Service
    Technology–Trade and
    Industry Division
7000 Dandini Boulevard
Sparks, Nevada 89512
(702) 673-7000

New Hampshire

New Hampshire Vocational
    Technical College
Culinary Arts
2020 Riverside Drive
Berlin, New Hampshire
    03570
(603) 752-1113

University of New Hampshire
    Thompson School of
    Applied Sciences
Food Service
    Management/Culinary
    Arts
Durham, New Hampshire
    03824
(603) 862-1025

New Jersey

Academy of Culinary Arts
    Atlantic Community
    College
Black Horse Pike
Mays Landing, New Jersey
    08330
(609) 625-1607

Atlantic Community College
    Hospitality Management
    Program
Mays Landing, New Jersey
    08330
(609) 625-1111

Bergen Community College
    Hotel/Restaurant
    Management Program
400 Paramus Road
Paramus, New Jersey 07652
(201) 447-1500

Brookdale Community
  College
Food Service Management
Newman Springs Road
Lincroft, New Jersey 07738
(201) 842-1900

Burlington County College
  Hospitality Management
  Pemberton Browns Mill
    Road
  Pemberton, New Jersey
    08068
  (609) 894-9511

Camden County College
  Dietetic Technician–Food
    Management
  Box 200B
  Blackwood, New Jersey
    08021
  (609) 227-7200

Career Center
  Cape May County
    Vocational Technical
    School
  Food Occupations
  Cresthaven Road
  Cape May Court House,
    New Jersey 08210
  (609) 465-2161

Hudson County Community
  College
  Culinary Arts
  161 Newkirk Street
  Jersey City, New Jersey
    07306
  (201) 656-2020

Middlesex County College
  Hotel, Restaurant and
    Institutional
    Management Department
  10 Mill Road
  Edison, New Jersey 08818
  (201) 548-6000

Ocean County College
  Food Service Management
  Toms River, New Jersey
    08753
  (201) 255-4000

Salem County Vocational
  Technical Schools
  Culinary Arts
  R.D. #2, Box 350
  Woodstown, New Jersey
    08098
  (609) 769-0101

New Mexico

Albuquerque Technical
     Vocational Institute
Culinary Arts
525 Buena Vista SE
Albuquerque, New Mexico
     87106
(505) 848-1700

New York

Adirondack Community
     College
Commercial
     Cooking/Occupational
     Education
Bay Road
Glens Falls, New York
     12801
(518) 793-4491

The Culinary Institute of
     America
Culinary Arts
P.O. Box 53
Hyde Park, New York 12538
(914) 452-9600

Erie Community College
Food Service
     Administration
Main and Youngs Road
Buffalo, New York 14221
(716) 634-0800

Fulton–Montgomery
     Community College
Food Service
     Administration
Route 67
Johnstown, New York
     12095
(518) 762-4651

Genesee Community College
Hospitality Management
One College Road
Batavia, New York 14020
(716) 343-0055

Herkimer County Community
     College
Food Service
     Administration
Reservoir Road
Herkimer, New York 13357
(315) 866-0300

Hudson Valley Community
College
Food Service
Administration
Department
80 Vandenburgh Avenue
Troy, New York 12180
(518) 283-1100

Jefferson Community College
Hospitality and Tourism
Outer Coffeen Street
Watertown, New York
13601
(315) 782-5250

Fiorello H. LaGuardia
Community College
Dietetic Technician Program
31-10 Thomson Avenue
Long Island City, New York
11101
(212) 626-5468

Mohawk Valley Community
College
Food Service
Floyd Avenue
Rome, New York 13440
(315) 339-3470

Monroe Community College
Food Service
Administration
100 E. Henrietta Road
Rochester, New York 14623
(716) 424-5200

Nassau Community College
Hotel/Restaurant
Management
Stewart Avenue
Garden City, New York
11530
(516) 222-7500

New York City Technical
College
Hotel and Restaurant
Management Department
300 Jay Street
Brooklyn, New York 11201
(212) 643-8386

New York Institute of Dietetics
Food and Hotel
Management
154 W. 14th Street
New York, New York 10011
(212) 675-6655

New York University
 Foodservice Management
  Program
 239 Greene Street, 537
  East Building
 New York, New York 10003
 (212) 598-2369

The New York Restaurant
  School
 The New School for Social
  Research
 27 W. 34th Street
 New York, New York 10001
 (212) 947-7097

Niagara County Community
  College
 Food Service/Professional
  Chef Option
 3111 Saunders Settlement
  Road
 Sanborn, New York 14132
 (716) 731-4101

Onondaga Community College
 Foodservice Administration
  and Hotel Management
 Route #173
 Syracuse, New York 13215
 (315) 469-7741

Schenectady County
  Community College
 Hotel Technology and
  Culinary Arts
 Washington Avenue
 Schenectady, New York
  12305
 (518) 346-6211

Paul Smith's College of Arts
  and Sciences
 Hotel/Restaurant
  Management and Chef
  Training
 Paul Smiths, New York
  12970
 (518) 327-6227

State University of New York
  at Alfred
 Food Service
 South Brooklyn Avenue
 Wellsville, New York 14895
 (607) 871-6215

State University of New York
  at Canton
 Hotel Technology,
  Restaurant Management
 Cornell Drive
 Canton, New York 13617
 (315) 386-7011

State University of New York
at Cobleskill
Food Service and
Hospitality
Administration
Champlin Hall
Cobleskill, New York 12043
(518) 234-5425

State University of New York
at Delhi
Hotel, Restaurant and Food
Service Management
Delhi, New York 13753
(607) 746-4189

State University of New York
at Farmingdale
Food Service
Administration/Restaurant
Management
Melville Road
Farmingdale, New York
11735
(516) 420-2000

State University of New York
at Morrisville
Food Science Technology
Bailey Annex
Morrisville, New York
13408
(315) 684-7016

Suffolk County Community
College
Dietetic Technician
Speonk Riverhead Road
Riverhead, New York 11901
(516) 369-2600

Sullivan County Community
College
Hotel Technology
Loch Sheldrake, New York
12759
(914) 434-5750

Tompkins Cortland
Community College
Hotel Technology/Food
Service Administration
170 North Street
Dryden, New York 13053
(607) 844-8211

Villa Maria College of Buffalo
Food Service Management
240 Pine Ridge Road
Buffalo, New York 14225
(716) 896-0700

Westchester Community
    College
Hotel and Restaurant
    Management
75 Grasslands Road
Valhalla, New York 10595
(914) 347-6959

North Carolina

Asheville Buncombe
    Technical College
Culinary Technology and
    Motel and Restaurant
    Management
340 Victoria Road
Asheville, North Carolina
    28801
(704) 254-1921

Central Piedmont Community
    College
Hotel, Restaurant
    Management Program
P.O. Box 35009
Charlotte, North Carolina
    28235
(704) 373-6721

Fayetteville Technical Institute
Food Service Management
P.O. Box 35236
Fayetteville, North Carolina
    28303
(919) 323-1961

Lenoir Community College
Food Service Management
P.O. Box 188
Kinston, North Carolina
    28502
(919) 527-6223

Southwestern Technical
    College
Food Service Management
P.O. Box 67
Sylva, North Carolina
    28779
(704) 586-4091

Wilkes Community College
Hotel/Restaurant
    Management
Drawer 120
Wilkesboro, North
    Carolina 28697
(919) 667-7136

North Dakota

Bismarck Junior College
Hotel, Motel and
  Restaurant Management
Shafer Heights
Bismarck, North Dakota
  58501
(701) 224-5479

North Dakota State School of
  Science
Cook and Chef Training
Wahpeton, North Dakota
  58075
(701) 671-2201

Ohio

Bowling Green State
  University
Applied Sciences
  Department
901 Rye Beach Road
Huron, Ohio 44839
(419) 433-5560

Cincinnati Technical College
Executive Chef
  Technology/Hotel–Motel–
  Restaurant Management
3520 Central Parkway
Cincinnati, Ohio 45223
(513) 861-9338

Clermont General and
  Technical College
University of Cincinnati
Hospitality Management
College Drive
Batavia, Ohio 45103
(513) 732-2990

Columbus Technical Institute
Hospitality Management
  Department
550 E. Spring Street
Columbus, Ohio 43215
(614) 227-2579

Cuyahoga Community College
Hospitality Management
2900 Community College
  Road
Cleveland, Ohio 44115
(216) 241-5966

Hocking Technical College
Hotel/Restaurant
Management
Route #1
Nelsonville, Ohio 45746
(614) 753-3591

Jefferson Technical College
Hospitality/Food Service
Management
4000 Sunset Boulevard
Steubenville, Ohio 43952
(614) 264-5591

Owens Technical College
Hospitality Management
Technology
30335 Oregon Road
Toledo, Ohio 43699
(419) 666-0580

Terra Technical College
Hospitality Management
1220 Cedar Street
Fremont, Ohio 43420
(419) 334-3886

University of
Toledo–Community and
Technical College
Food Service
Management/Culinary
Arts
W. Bancroft Street
Toledo, Ohio 43606
(419) 537-3112

Youngstown State University
Food and Nutrition/Dietetics
410 Wick Avenue
Youngstown, Ohio 44555
(216) 742-3344

Oklahoma

Carl Albert Junior College
School of Hotel and
Restaurant Management
P.O. Box 606
Poteau, Oklahoma 74953
(918) 647-8221

Great Plains Area Vocational
Technical Center
Commercial Food
Services/Fast Foods
Management
4500 W. Lee Boulevard
Lawton, Oklahoma 73505
(405) 355-6371

Indian Meridian Vocational
Technical School
Commercial Food
Production and
Management
1312 S. Sangre Road
Stillwater, Oklahoma 74074
(405) 377-3333

Oklahoma State University
School of Technical
Training
Food Service
Fourth and Mission
Okmulgee, Oklahoma
74447
(918) 756-6211

Pioneer Area Vocational
Technical School
Commercial Foods
2101 N. Ash
Ponca City, Oklahoma
74601
(405) 762-8336

Southern Oklahoma Area
Vocational–Technical
School
Culinary Arts
Route 1
Ardmore, Oklahoma 73401
(405) 223-2070

Tulsa Junior College
Lodging and Food Service
Management
909 S. Boston
Tulsa, Oklahoma 74119
(918) 587-6561

Oregon

Chemeketa Community
College
Food Service Management
P.O. Box 14007
Salem, Oregon 97309
(503) 399-5091

Lane Community College
Food Service Management
4000 E. 30th Avenue
Eugene, Oregon 97405
(503) 747-4501

Linn–Benton Community
College
Culinary Arts/Restaurant
Management
6500 S.W. Pacific
Boulevard
Albany, Oregon 97321
(503) 928-2361

Portland Community College
Hotel/Motel or Restaurant
Management/Sous Chef
12000 S.W. 49th
Portland, Oregon 97219
(503) 244-6111

Pennsylvania

Community College of
    Allegheny County
Hospitality
    Management/Culinary
    Arts
595 Beatty Road
Monroeville, Pennsylvania
    15146
(412) 327-1327

Bucks County Community
    College
Hotel, Motel and
    Institutional
    Management/Culinary
    Arts
Swamp Road
Newtown, Pennsylvania
    18940
(215) 968-8225

Butler County Community
    College
Food Service Management
Oak Hills, College Drive
Butler, Pennsylvania 16001
(412) 287-8711

Delaware County Community
    College
Hotel/Restaurant
    Management
Route 252
Media, Pennsylvania 19063
(215) 353-5400

Harrisburg Area Community
    College
Food Service Management
3300 Cameron Street
Harrisburg, Pennsylvania
    17110
(717) 780-2493

Keystone Junior College
Hospitality Management
La Plume, Pennsylvania
    18440
(717) 945-5141

Luzerne County Community
    College
Hotel and Restaurant
    Management
Prospect Street and Middle
    Road
Nanticoke, Pennsylvania
    18634
(717) 735-8300

Montgomery County
  Community College
  Hospitality Management
  Program
  340 DeKalb Pike
  Blue Bell, Pennsylvania
  19422
  (215) 643-6000

Peirce Junior College
  Hospitality Management
  1420 Pine Street
  Philadelphia, Pennsylvania
  19102
  (215) 545-6400

Pennsylvania State University,
  Berks Campus
  Hotel and Food Service
  College of Human
  Development
  R.D. #5, Tulpehocken Road
  Reading, Pennsylvania
  19608
  (215) 375-4211

Community College of
  Philadelphia
  Hotel, Restaurant and
  Institutional Management
  1700 Spring Garden Road
  Philadelphia, Pennsylvania
  19130
  (215) 751-8704

The Restaurant School
  Restaurant
  Management/Chef
  Training
  2129 Walnut Street
  Philadelphia, Pennsylvania
  19103
  (215) 561-3446

Westmoreland County
  Community College
  Food Service
  Management/Culinary
  Arts
  Armbrust Road
  Youngwood, Pennsylvania
  15697
  (412) 925-4000

Williamsport Area
  Community College
  Food and Hospitality
  Management
  1005 W. Third Street
  Williamsport, Pennsylvania
  17701
  (717) 326-3761

Rhode Island

Johnson and Wales College
Hotel
    Management/Culinary
    Arts
8 Abbott Park Place
Providence, Rhode Island
    02903
(401) 456-1000

South Carolina

Greenville Technical College
Food Science
P.O. Box 5616, Station
    "B"
Greenville, South Carolina
    29606
(803) 242-3170

Horry–Georgetown Technical
    College
Hotel, Motel and
    Restaurant Management
Highway 501 East, P.O.
    Box 1966
Conway, South Carolina
    29526
(803) 347-3186

University of South Carolina
Hotel, Restaurant and
    Tourism Administration
084 Coliseum, District A-1
Columbia, South Carolina
    29208
(803) 777-6665

South Dakota

Black Hills State College
Travel Industry Management
1200 University
Spearfish, South Dakota
    57783
(605) 642-6734

Mitchell Area Vocational
    Technical School
Cook/Chef
821 N. Capitol
Mitchell, South Dakota
    57301
(605) 996-6671

Tennessee

Knoxville State Area
   Vocational Technical
   School
Commercial Food
   Preparation
1100 Liberty Street
Knoxville, Tennessee 37919
(615) 546-5567

Nashville Area Vocational
   Technical School
Commercial Foods
2601 Bransford Avenue
Nashville, Tennessee 37207
(615) 254-9718

Shelby State Community
   College
Department of Nutrition
   and Dietetics
P.O. Box 40568
Memphis, Tennessee 38104
(901) 528-6865

State Technical Institute at
   Memphis
Motel/Restaurant
   Management Technology
5983 Macon Cove
Memphis, Tennessee 38184
(901) 377-4132

Texas

Central Texas College
Food Service and
   Hotel/Motel Management
Highway 190 West
Killeen, Texas 76542
(817) 526-1248

Del Mar College
Restaurant Management
   Department
Baldwin at Ayers
Corpus Christi, Texas 78404
(512) 881-6435

El Centro College
Food Service Operations
Main at Lamar Streets
Dallas, Texas 75202
(214) 746-2202

Hill Junior College
Food Preparation, Service
   and Management
Box 619
Hillsboro, Texas 76645
(817) 582-2555

Houston Community College
Culinary Arts
1300 Holman
Houston, Texas 77004
(713) 521-0046

Houston Community College
  Hotel, Restaurant, Club
    Management
  4310 Dunlavy
  Houston, Texas 77006
  (713) 868-0775

Northwood Institute–Texas
  Hotel/Restaurant
    Management
  P.O. Box 58 FR 1382
  Cedar Hill, Texas 75401
  (214) 291-1541

St. Phillips College
  Hospitality
    Management/Chefs
    Apprenticeship
  2111 Nevada
  San Antonio, Texas 78203
  (512) 531-3315

San Jacinto College–North
    Campus
  Restaurant Management
    and Dietetic Technology
  8060 Spencer Highway
  Pasadena, Texas 77505
  (713) 476-1869

South Plains
    College–Lubbock
  Food Industry Management
  1302 Main Street
  Lubbock, Texas 79401
  (806) 747-0576

Texas State Technical Institute
  Food Service Technology
    Program
  Building 15-1
  Waco, Texas 76705
  (817) 799-3611

Utah

Utah Technical College
  Hotel–Motel/Restaurant
    Management
  P.O. Box 1609
  Provo, Utah 84601
  (801) 226-5000

Vermont

Ethan Allen Community
    College
  Hotel/Restaurant
    Management
  310 Bonnet Street
  Manchester Center,
    Vermont 05255
  (802) 362-3588

Champlain College
  Hotel, Motel and
    Restaurant Management
  232 S. Willard Street
  Burlington, Vermont 05402
  (802) 658-0800

New England Culinary
 Institute
Culinary Arts
110 E. State Street
Montpelier, Vermont 05602
(802) 229-4445

Virginia

Thomas Nelson Community
 College
Hotel, Restaurant and
 Institutional Management
P.O. Box 9407
Hampton, Virginia 23670
(804) 825-2900

Northern Virginia
 Community College
Hotel, Restaurant and
 Institutional Management
8333 Little River Turnpike
Annandale, Virginia 22003
(703) 323-3457

Tidewater Community College
Hotel, Restaurant and
 Institutional Management
1700 College Crescent
Virginia Beach, Virginia
 23456
(804) 427-3070

John Tyler Community
 College
Food Service Management
Chester, Virginia 23831
(804) 796-4031

Washington

Clark College
Culinary Arts
1800 East McLoughlin
 Boulevard
Vancouver, Washington
 98663
(206) 699-0143

Everett Community College
Food Technology
801 Wetmore Avenue
Everett, Washington 98201
(206) 259-7151

Fort Steilacoom Community
 College
Food Service Management
P.O. Box 33265
Fort Lewis, Washington
 98433
(206) 964-6567

Highline Community College
Hospitality and Tourism
Management
Pacific Highway South and
South 240th
Midway, Washington 98032
(206) 878-3710

North Seattle Community
College
Restaurant
Management/Culinary
Arts
9600 College Way North
Seattle, Washington 98103
(206) 634-4503

Olympic College
Commercial Cooking/Food
Service
16th and Chester
Bremerton, Washington
98310
(206) 478-4576

Seattle Central Community
College.
Hospitality
Management/Culinary
Arts
1702 Harvard Avenue
Seattle, Washington 98122
(206) 587-5424

Shoreline Community College
Food Services Technology
16101 Greenwood Avenue
North
Seattle, Washington 98133
(206) 546-4789

Skagit Valley College
Culinary Arts/Restaurant
Management
2405 College Way
Mount Vernon, Washington
98273
(206) 428-1211

South Seattle Community
College
Food Service
Management/Pastry and
Specialty Baking
6000 16th Avenue S.W.
Seattle, Washington 98106
(206) 764-5344

Spokane Community College
Culinary Arts/Hotel–Motel
Management
1810 N. Green Street
Spokane, Washington 99207
(509) 535-0642

West Virginia

Fairmont Community College
Food Service Management
Home
    Economics/Technology
Fairmont, West Virginia
    26554
(304) 367-4271

Garnet Career Center
Commercial Foods
422 Dickinson Street
Charleston, West Virginia
    25301
(304) 348-6127

James Rumsey Vocational
    Technical Center
Food Service Occupations
Route 6, Box 268
Martinsburg, West Virginia
    25401
(304) 754-7925

Shepherd College
Hotel, Motel and
    Restaurant Management
Shepherdstown, West
    Virginia 25443
(304) 876-2511

West Virginia State College
Hotel, Restaurant and
    Institutional Management
Campus Box 53
Institute, West Virginia
    25112
(304) 766-3118

Wisconsin

District 1 Technical Institute
Restaurant and Hotel
    Cookery; Hospitality
    Management
620 W. Clairemont Avenue
Eau Claire, Wisconsin
    54701
(715) 836-3907

Fox Valley Technical Institute
Home and Consumer
    Sciences Division
1825 North Bluemound
    Drive
Appleton, Wisconsin 54913
(414) 735-5722

Gateway Technical Institute
Hotel/Motel Management;
    Food Service Management
1001 S. Main Street
Racine, Wisconsin 53403
(414) 631-7300

Madison Area Technical
    College
Industrial Foods
211 N. Carroll Street
Madison, Wisconsin 53703
(608) 266-5007

Milwaukee Area Technical
    College
Restaurant and Hotel
    Cookery Program
1015 N. Sixth Street
Milwaukee, Wisconsin
    53203
(414) 278-6255

Moraine Park Technical
    Institute
Restaurant and Hotel
    Cookery
235 N. National Avenue
Fond du Lac, Wisconsin
    54935
(414) 922-8611

Nicolet College
Hospitality Management
Box 518
Rhinelander, Wisconsin
    54501
(715) 369-4410

Southwest Wisconsin
    Vocational Technical
    Institute
Food Service Management
Route #1, Box 500
Fennimore, Wisconsin
    53809
(608) 822-3262

Western Wisconsin Technical
    Institute
Food Service Management
Eighth and Pine Streets
LaCrosse, Wisconsin 54601
(608) 785-9267

Wisconsin Indianhead
    Technical Institute
Hospitality
    Management–Tourism
2100 Beaser Avenue
Ashland, Wisconsin 54806
(715) 682-4591

Wyoming

Laramie County Community
    College
Food Service
1400 E. College Drive
Cheyenne, Wyoming 82007
(307) 634-5853

WHERE TO WRITE FOR MORE INFORMATION

The following is a list of associations to contact for further information on opportunities in restaurant careers.

National Restaurant Association
Information Service and Library
1200 17th Street, N.W.
Washington, DC 20036

The Education Foundation of the National Restaurant Association
250 S. Wacker Drive
Suite 1400
Chicago, IL 60606

American Culinary Federation
Educational Institute
P.O. Box 3466
St. Augustine, FL 32084

Culinary Institute of America
P.O. Box 53
Hyde Park
New York, NY 12528

Council on Hotel, Restaurant and Institutional Education
   Human Development Building
   Room 118
   University Park, PA 16802

The American Dietetic Association
   208 S. LaSalle Street
   Chicago, IL 60604

The American Hotel and Motel Association
   888 Seventh Avenue
   New York, NY 10106

Dietary Managers Association
   4410 W. Roosevelt Road
   Hillside, IL 60162

A good source of information also includes local employers, your individual state employment services, any of the schools listed in appendix A, and trade periodicals such as the following:

Food Management
   747 Third Avenue
   New York, NY 10017

Restaurant Business
   633 Third Avenue
   New York, NY 10017

Nation's Restaurant News
   425 Park Avenue
   New York, NY 10017

Restaurants and Institutions
   Cahners Plaza
   1350 Touhy Avenue
   P.O. Box 5080
   Des Plaines, IL 60017

Career Grant   C1